MORE THAN I CAN BEAR IF NOT FOR
GOD

Dr. Philemon Topas, PhD

WESTBOW
PRESS®
A DIVISION OF THOMAS NELSON
& ZONDERVAN

All Scripture quotations, unless otherwise indicated, are taken from the Holy Bible, New International Version®, NIV®. Copyright ©1973, 1978, 1984, 2011 by Biblica, Inc.™ Used by permission of Zondervan. All rights reserved worldwide. www.zondervan.com The "NIV" and "New International Version" are trademarks registered in the United States Patent and Trademark Office by Biblica, Inc.™

Scripture taken from the King James Version of the Bible.

WestBow Press books may be ordered through booksellers or by contacting:

WestBow Press
A Division of Thomas Nelson & Zondervan
1663 Liberty Drive
Bloomington, IN 47403
www.westbowpress.com
1 (866) 928-1240

ISBN: 978-1-9736-3932-9 (sc)
ISBN: 978-1-9736-3931-2 (hc)
ISBN: 978-1-9736-3933-6 (e)

Library of Congress Control Number: 2018910808

Print information available on the last page.

WestBow Press rev. date: 9/24/2018

I dedicate this book to my dear wife, Luba, who made love meaningful to me and our four children. Thanks for giving me the courage to stay focused in adversity.

To my four children, Naomi, Zevin, Jael and Marko, your zeal and dedication to the Word of God in the midst of adversity inspired your mom and me. Remain blessed.

To my late mom and dad, whose sacrifice, hard work and love for the Bible taught me and my seven siblings to honour and serve God; my late sister and my late nephew, whose companionship enriched my life; and my late father-in-law for his generosity and support during our times of need. I missed the burials and funerals for all of you, but I know we will see each other again. Rest in peace.

To all the friends, pastors, professors and research fellows who encouraged me and continue to teach me about the love that overcomes trial and difficulties, thank you.

To every believer and unbeliever going through trials and difficulties, I pray you continue to rely on and seek help from God, respectively.

To my Lord and Saviour, Jesus Christ, who is the solid rock on which my family and I stand, be glorified. Amen.

Contents

Preface

This book is about my educational studies at five academic and research institutions that trained and equipped me for a professional career in entomology. Sadly, because of a crisis beyond human tolerance in my life, I was unable to realize my dream of having a productive career. My ordeal started with the sudden onset of eye problems and inflammation of my lymph nodes shortly after I had knee surgery at the University of Flatland Hospital in January 1983. Subsequently, the immigration department used my health problems to declare that I was inadmissible to Multizone. The department mistreated me prior to my becoming a citizen of Multizone.

Briefly, I am blind in one eye, and I have substantial loss of vision in the other eye. I had 20/20 vision in both eyes prior to my knee surgery. I have also developed a plethora of health conditions that significantly limit my respiratory, ambulatory and other vital functions. It is not easy for me to talk about my medical ordeal. The expectation of finding a solution through dialogue and legal channels was a major contributor to the 20 years it took to write this book. Nevertheless, my moral obligations to society compel me to make the public aware of the hurdles I encounter in my effort to receive compensation and have closure to my nightmare.

When my ordeal started, I was 30 years old and married, and my wife and I were expecting our first child. I am 66 years old this year, 2018. My 36 pressure-filled years of unemployment have taken a toll on my family. My efforts to resolve the ordeal at the regional and national levels of government and through legal means have all been fruitless. My family and I have suffered immeasurable damages. My wife has had several mental breakdowns and is on medication to manage depression.

Our 35-year-old elder daughter is mentally delayed due to a head injury she suffered soon after she was delivered at the University of Flatland Hospital in May 1983. We are devastated. Our faith and belief in God continue to sustain us. We are grateful to God for his faithfulness toward us.

Three of our four children reside in different cities in Grandonia. My wife, our elder daughter, and I reside in Looney Bay, Multizone. My wife and I are still unemployed despite being well qualified and making countless attempts and applications for employment. I was a postdoctoral fellow at Shoreline University in Redberry, Shoreline. I have a PhD in aquatic entomology from the University of Flatland in Dusty Rose. My wife earned a bachelor's degree in education from the same university. My master of science degree in agricultural entomology is from Amicus University, Luxville. The University of Nugget River in Noogle awarded my bachelor of science degree in zoology and botany. I also earned a diploma in vector-borne disease control from Needlepoint, Jasper. I am currently collecting a meagre amount of old-age pension because I barely worked. We have no other sources of income, and my daughter is on disability income.

In conclusion, justice has eluded my family and me. It hurts that we are still waiting for justice in a democratic nation like Multizone. Presently, life is overwhelming to us. It would be more than we could bear if not for God. My daughter's and my needs would be better met with proper legal and medical assistance. I have limited income and resources to pay for such help.

Acknowledgments

Endeavours that contribute to the advancement of knowledge, wisdom and understanding are usually achieved through collaborative efforts.

The ideas, editing and typing skill of my gorgeous wife and comrade made significant improvement to the contents of this book. I owe her tons of gratitude.

The love, patience and encouragement of my wife and our four children enabled me to have the time, space and desire to complete this book. I am grateful to them.

CHAPTER 1
Life in Nugget River

Preuniversity Education in Nugget River

Sunset on October 14, 1976, was beautiful. I sat on a patch of grass behind the administration building of the University of Nugget River in Beaufort and watched the gigantic arc of the crimson sun descend below the horizon. The beauty of the sunset temporarily diverted my attention from a thought that had occupied my mind for a couple of weeks. I was expecting a letter the next morning, and it was going to bring relief or anguish to the thought. I went back to my laboratory in the zoology department after watching the sunset, and I fed my snails.

Dr. Ziggler, who was the chairman of department, and I were cooperating on a project that involved the effect of photo period on the growth and reproduction of edible snails. I could have spent more time in the laboratory, working on other aspects of the snail project, but my mind was too distracted by the thought.

I left the laboratory and went home for dinner. My mother made one of my favourite dishes for dinner: fried plantain and black-eyed bean stew. Under normal circumstances, I would have consumed more than my usual share, but not on that evening. Anxiety and nervousness adversely affected my appetite. I had to force myself to stay calm. I managed to finish only a portion of my dinner.

I went to bed at nine o'clock, an hour earlier than my usual bedtime, in an attempt to hide my anxiety and nervousness from my family. It was a good strategy, but it was one my mother saw through. She came to my room at about ten o'clock and told me to relax and have a good sleep. She knew that the next morning, I would learn the response to my interview for a scholarship to pursue graduate studies in entomology at Amicus University in Luxville, Multizone.

We talked for about 15 minutes, and I confided in her, as I had done a countless number of times since my childhood. I told her I was not sure I could handle not being awarded the scholarship. She knew I was eager and determined to pursue graduate studies in Multizone. We also talked about religion, and she reminded me that as a child of God, I should cast all my cares on him. Finally, she wished me luck as she closed my bedroom door behind her.

It was about one o'clock in the morning when I finally fell asleep. In the interim, I thought about the various options available to me in case I was not awarded the scholarship. The department of zoology at the University of Nugget River had expressed interest in admitting me to the master of science (MS) program in entomology. I also thought of working for a year in the zoology department or outside the university before pursuing graduate studies. My preference, nevertheless, was to continue with my studies at Amicus University. Without the scholarship, the latter option was unattainable.

Morning came quickly, perhaps because I went to bed late and was up by six o'clock in the morning. I went jogging at seven o'clock, primarily to refresh myself. I also wanted to be alone so I could mentally prepare myself for the important event later that morning. After breakfast, I waited expectantly and nervously for the special mail to be delivered to the local post office. My younger sister went to the post office and collected the mail at ten o'clock. I waited outside the house for her. When I saw her coming with the mail, the rate of my heartbeat increased. The closer she came to our house, the faster my heart beat. I could hardly wait to collect the mail from her. Despite my anxiety and nervousness, I managed to thank her. I grabbed the mail from her with my shaky and sweaty hands. Voila! There was the letter that had virtually driven me nuts for the past couple weeks. I tossed every other piece of mail aside and took a deep breath of fresh air—and then fear seized me. I was scared to open the letter. At that instant, I closed my eyes and offered a brief prayer to God to give me the courage to accept whatever decision the scholarships secretariat had made. When I opened the letter, the first word that caught my eye was *Congratulations*. Further reading confirmed I had been awarded the scholarship.

My mother was the first to congratulate me. She told me she had been sure I was going to be awarded the scholarship. We had a family party that evening to celebrate my success. When the party was over, I went for a walk around my jogging route. It was a pleasant evening, with a gentle breeze that made the leaves rustle quietly. I was happy to be alone. I spent much of the time on the walk thinking about what life at Amicus University was going to be like.

I'd acquired most of my knowledge of the educational system in Upper Contica at that time from the library at the University of Nugget River. I'd also learned about specific colleges and universities, including Amicus, from the library at the Grandonian consulate in Beaufort, the capital city of Nugget River. Television, radio and news magazines were also useful sources of information. I knew that the system of education in Multizone and Grandonia was not structured like the Derkland system, which I was used to. The academic year at the University of Nugget River was composed of three semesters instead of two, unlike at the universities and colleges of Multizone and Grandonia. The final examination at the end of the third semester was an all-or-nothing affair with regard to the grade for that academic year. Assignments and tests done during the semester contributed little to determine the final grade. I knew that Multizone had two official languages. I knew also that English was the official language of instruction at Amicus, despite the fact that the university was located in the midst of the largest community that spoke Multizone's other official language.

My knowledge of Multizone's other official language was passable. I had studied that language in secondary school in Nugget River for five years. I'd scored a passing grade on the final examination. I knew enough of that language to engage in conversation. Photographs and movies of various seasonal festivals had taught me much about the variety of seasonal activities common to both Grandonia and Multizone. I was eager to see and touch snow and experience what winter was like. Hockey, to me, was splendid and magical. I'd learned about the dynamics of skating in my advanced-level physics class. I couldn't wait to see a hockey game or go to a skating rink. I had seen movies and photographs of the winter carnival in Neauville. I knew there was a lot more to learn and discover about life in Upper Contica, especially in Multizone.

The walk was refreshing. It gave me the opportunity to think about the award and the door it had opened for me to continue with my educational career. I went to bed early that evening. I needed to catch up on the sleep I had missed the previous night. The events of the day occupied my mind as I lay in bed. On the one hand, I was glad I'd been awarded the scholarship. On the other hand, I was sad about leaving my family and Gondwana. I went to sleep knowing I had nine months to resolve most of the questions on my mind. Amicus was not expecting me until September 1977.

I had a relaxing sleep, unlike the previous night. I woke up late the following morning. I called my supervisor and asked to take the rest of the week off from my research work at the university. Luckily, he agreed. The week after I received the award, I began planning the myriad of things I had to do in the months preceding my departure to Amicus. The first thing on my agenda was to submit duplicate copies of medical examination results to the Multizonian embassy in Nugget River. I had to submit the paperwork at least eight months prior to my departure date. The Multizonian embassy required enough time for immigration doctors in Looney Bay to review the results. The next item was to make arrangements for various immunization shots. The other urgent item on my list was to take the Graduate Record Examinations (GRE) and the Test of English as a Foreign Language (TOEFL). Amicus University wanted the results of both examinations prior to my departure for Multizone. The Grandonian consulate in Nugget River administered both tests on behalf of the examination board in Neewton, Grandonia. I made plans to take both tests early in case I did not do well and needed to repeat one or both tests. The arrangement for a Nugget River passport was another urgent and important thing on my agenda. In the midst of maintaining a hectic schedule of research at the university and making arrangements for my departure, I managed to find time to think about my preparedness for life in Multizone.

I knew without a shadow of a doubt that I would have to make adjustments to my social calendar. Being away from home and my family was nothing new to me. I'd gone to a Christian boarding school when I was 14 years old. I'd visited home once or twice a month. It had been difficult at first. I'd missed the family atmosphere, including the quarrels and occasional fights with my sisters. Most importantly, I'd missed home-cooked food. Eventually, I'd gotten used to the environment at the boarding school.

Initially, life at the boarding school was difficult. We got up every morning five o'clock to perform chores. We took turns moving from one chore to another. I hated cleaning the toilets and ironing school uniforms. I found it hard to see the relevance of ironing one's uniform. Nevertheless, I had to perform the latter two chores with precision to avoid disciplinary action. When our chores were done, we had to jog for two miles and exercise for 15 minutes. I made it a habit as often as I could to sneak to a river close to the boarding school after exercising. It was a welcoming and replenishing swim whenever I could go. I enjoyed swimming early in the morning. The initial shock of the cold water was a relief to me. After I acclimatized to the water's temperature, it became pleasant and fun to be in. It was a welcome relief to swim and watch the golden reflection of the morning sun from the surface of the river some distance away. I usually made it back to campus in time for the morning inspection of our beds, uniforms and chores.

Breakfast was followed by morning worship. It was compulsory to attend the morning and other devotional activities. Nugget River was a former colony of Derkland, but the Kilan region of the country where I was born once had been colonized by Allemagnia. One of the legacies the Allemagnian colonizers had left behind was the Presbyterian church. Church services at the boarding school were strictly after the Presbyterian order. I enjoyed the morning devotions and hated the Saturday and Sunday evening devotional hours. Nevertheless, the formative years of my Christian upbringing benefited immensely from the Christian environment at the boarding school. Academically, the school's curriculum was rewarding. There were compulsory hours for homework and other academic activities. It was mandatory to spend time in the library daily to be able to submit weekly critical articles on new publications on selected topics. I either had to mature and endure the hard and tedious training or withdraw from the boarding school.

It was common for students to attempt to run away when the pressure became unbearable. Such bold attempts were usually met with strict disciplinary action. I graduated from the boarding school and proceeded to secondary school in 1965.

Life at the secondary school was fine. The training I'd received at the boarding school had prepared me for the social and academic atmosphere at the secondary school. The first secondary school I attended was eight hours by bus from home. After my first year, I transferred to another secondary school that was closer to my hometown. Apart from proximity, a couple of other major contributing factors made it necessary for me to transfer.

My elder and younger sisters attended the latter school, and my parents wanted the three of us to be together. The academic program and extracurricular activities were also better at my sisters' school. After four years at my new school, I wrote the high school equivalent examination in June 1970. My grades were good enough to enable me to earn an academic scholarship for a two-year advanced-level program at the same school. Some of my classmates gained admission to other Nugget River schools for their advanced-level programs.

We had eight new students from other schools in our advanced-level class. Three of my close Christian friends were among the students in my advanced-level class. I was particularly excited to see the latter group of friends. The joy of seeing my Christian friends again overshadowed my initial delight about my academic success. Apart from being classmates, we also belonged to the Student Christian Fellowship organization on campus. We worshipped together every Friday evening and had dusk-to-dawn prayer and fellowship meetings once a month. Needless to say, the fellowship was a vital source of spiritual growth in my budding Christian life. At one of our fellowship meetings in 1968, I committed my life to Christ and became a born-again Christian. We reorganized, and over a few weeks, we got serious with the fellowship meetings. The Lord moved mightily in that fellowship. As a member of the executive, I devoted a considerable amount of time to organizing meetings. Some of my most beneficial and joyous times in secondary school were our weekly fellowship meetings. The fellowship contributed substantially to my Christian maturity and helped me to develop a personal relationship with God.

The discipline I acquired as a Christian also helped in my academic work. I had to be careful and disciplined about how I managed my time during my advanced-level program. Apart from being involved in the organization of fellowship activities, I was also made the sports captain in the first year of my two-year program. The latter responsibility was demanding on my time. I was in charge of all sporting activities on campus. Representatives of the various sporting activities helped me in discharging my duties, yet I still spent a substantial amount of time on meetings on and off the campus, especially during sports festivals and competitions. Amid my involvement in a myriad of extracurricular activities, I managed to stay on course with my academic work. I had to maintain good grades for my scholarship to be renewed. The award paid for a substantial portion of my tuition, housing and food. Losing the scholarship would have derailed my academic career. My parents had been expelled from Nugget River in 1970, the same year I gained admission to the advanced-level program.

Nugget River had serious economic problems due to a deep global recession in 1970. In order to deal with the problems, the government of Nugget River expelled all the legal and illegal aliens from the country. My parents had legally migrated to Nugget River from Kolaland just before the beginning of the last world war. Two of my elder sisters were born in Kolaland. Five other siblings and I were born in Nugget River. I was the only male child until 1962, when my younger brother, Timothy, was born. We grew up in Nugget River and were fluent in three of the myriad languages spoken in Nugget River, in addition to Ayama, my parents' native language.

The expulsion of my parents destabilized our family. My parents left my elder and younger sisters and me behind. They were concerned about our education and did not want to relocate us to Kolaland in the midst of the expulsion and confusion. The government of Nugget River allowed the expelled aliens to take only the barest necessities. Most of the money they had saved and other assets were either frozen or confiscated. In some regions of Nugget River, the shops and businesses of wealthy people from Kolaland were looted. The ensuing stress and frustration of the expulsion led some of the expelled aliens to commit suicide. The government of Kolaland supplied the expelled aliens with food and accommodation when they were expelled. The sudden influx of about three million aliens from Nugget River was more than the government of Kolaland could handle. Several attempts by the government of Kolaland to retrieve aliens' assets from Nugget River were fruitless. A few of the expelled aliens received some of their savings from the Branch of Dealer Bank in Kolaland. When the going got worse, my parents left Kolaland and relocated to Aurus. Proximity to my two sisters and me and a better opportunity to start a new business were the major motivational factors in their decision to settle in Aurus.

My parents visited and sent us allowances regularly. We spent most of our vacations with my elder sister's boyfriend, and whenever it was possible, we went to my parents' in Aurus. The expulsion and its aftermath affected the performance of the three of us in school. It was difficult to concentrate on our studies, especially in the first couple months after my parents' sudden departure. The first vacation was particularly devastating. My elder sister's boyfriend had just started working. There was barely enough room for all of us in his two-bed room apartment. He was generous. He made us feel at home; nevertheless, there was uneasiness and tension, especially at bedtime. I am grateful to him for his help. Things would have been more difficult without his assistance. He even sent us allowances when we went back to school, during breaks and in between semesters.

My grades were good enough after the first year of my advanced-level program to retain my scholarship for the second and final year. I had excellent grades in chemistry and physics. My biology grade met the required standard but could have been better with more effort. I missed a few laboratory and lecture classes when I travelled to Aurus to visit my mother in the hospital. She suffered from asthma, and her illness had flared up. The attack was severe enough that my dad asked my sisters and me to come to Aurus. We remained in Aurus for another week after she was discharged from hospital after a week of intensive care. My final year of the advanced-level program was rugged compared to the first year.

I wrote my final examination in March and April of 1972. The results were not as encouraging and satisfactory as I would have liked. My grades were not good enough to be admitted to the first-year bachelor of science program by the three universities in Nugget River. Naturally, I was disappointed. It was the first time I had failed a major examination. I went through all sorts of emotions and was sleepless for several nights. It was difficult to see my close friends leave for university to pursue their careers. I am grateful to my two sisters who helped me survive those bitter and sour days. My sisters suggested I go visit the rest of the family in Aurus. I heeded their advice and went on an extended vacation in Aurus. Family members in Aurus were also disappointed yet sympathetic about the outcome of my final examination. I was glad I went to visit them. Spending time with them, especially helping my dad in his new business, gave me much-needed relief from my thoughts about my final examination. I had the option to rewrite the examination, and my parents encouraged me to do so.

I returned to Nugget River after spending a month with my parents and applied for a job at the Public Services Commission in Beaufort. I was employed as an assistant to one of the executive officers. Initially, it was difficult for me to combine eight hours of work with studying. When I returned home, I was usually too tired to concentrate on my studies. I had eight months to prepare. I knew that was enough time for me if I could settle down and follow my studying schedule. I registered for part-time courses at the local workers' college and spent most of my weekends at the University of Nugget River's library. I also took advantage of the proximity of the university to visit my former classmates and some professors on campus. Both of my sisters went to work after obtaining their high school equivalent certificates; thus, we were able to rent an apartment close to the University of Nugget River.

The University of Nugget River

I rewrote the university qualifying examination in April 1973. I received better grades the second time around in biology and physics. My cumulative grades earned me admission to the bachelor of science program in the faculty of science at the University of Nugget River in 1973. I was no stranger to the campus. I knew my way around, and I was particularly excited to be housed in Noogle Hall. Among the four residences on campus in 1973, Noogle had the most gentlemanly and well-behaved students. Most of my former advanced-level classmates who'd been admitted the previous year lived in Noogle Hall. Our reunion was enhanced by proximity, and old bonds of friendship were easily revived. I would have been unhappy to be in Haggard Hall. The latter hall had the dubious reputation of being the Hall of Vandals. Students in Haggard Hall were called vandals because they worshipped Bacchus, the Roman god of wine. A yearly 12-hour alcohol binge accompanied by choruses of obscene songs was devoted to celebrating Bacchus's birthday. Some of the songs were so foul and vulgar that those who sang them wore masks for disguise. Kilan Hall was the female housing, and Benedict Hall, another calm and well-behaved hall, was for coed housing.

I was scarcely on campus during the first week. I visited my sisters in the evenings and spent the weekends at home. I was used to eating home-cooked food and staying with my sister. It took a couple of weeks for me to settle down on campus.

The University of Nugget River was well designed. The university had been built when Nugget River was a Derkland colony, and Derkland architects had done the design and supervision during construction of most of the buildings. It was a beautiful campus with luscious vegetation, trees and flowers, except in the cold months of December and January. The spacious and extensive arboretum on campus was a model of botanical beauty. The arboretum was well kept and groomed jointly by the department of botany and the maintenance department. Visitors from all over Beaufort, the capital city of Nugget River, came to the arboretum on weekends. It was also a tourist attraction for other citizens of Nugget River and foreigners. The fishless pond at the southern end of the arboretum was surrounded by different species of aquatic plants and wildflowers. The mating calls of the species of frogs in the pond merged into a chorus that could be deafening some evenings and nights. The firefly lane was my favourite part of the arboretum at night. I have hitherto not seen such a dense aggregation of fireflies. A path through the vegetation was usually illuminated by the brightness of the light emitted by the hundreds of thousands of fireflies that inhabited it, hence the name firefly lane. It was impossible to walk the firefly lane without the flies landing on one's clothing. They were easy to spot and remove once one was in darkness. The arboretum was also home to several fruit trees. Mangoes were abundant when in season. I made it a habit to change my jogging path and go through the arboretum when mangoes were in season, to pick a few for breakfast and a snack after lunch. Oranges, grapefruit, dates, pawpaws and several other tropical fruits were also present in the arboretum. Whenever I needed to be alone, the arboretum provided a perfect paradise for me. I was an executive member of the University Christian Fellowship, and we organized several retreats to the arboretum on weekends. In addition to the arboretum, each residence had open-air ponds and fountains decorated with beautiful aquatic vegetation. The campus also had several other parks and walking paths.

The University of Nugget River needed such a landscape for relaxation from the intense and vigorous academic work. The university had the reputation as a place for a special breed of students referred to as bookworms. The academic load was heavy. Each student admitted to the University of Nugget River was on a government scholarship. The scholarship was renewable on a yearly basis, depending on satisfactory academic performance. I was in the guinea-pig freshman class of 1973. Our freshman class was the start of the replacement of the four-year BS and BA degrees with a three-year honours program. On the one hand, I knew the change would be academically demanding and shorten our vacation time. On the other hand, I was glad I would be able to graduate with my colleagues who'd gone to the University of Nugget River the previous year. The academic load for the three-year program was as heavy as I had expected. I still remember the dreaded six-hour organic chemistry laboratory sections. My other subjects were physics with mathematics, zoology and botany. Gondwana studies was mandatory for all first-year students. Ghosting, or studying between midnight and three o'clock in the morning, was not prohibited at the University of Nugget River. We had not been allowed to study at such late hours at the Christian boarding school. I took full advantage of ghosting on the days I had no morning classes. I was on the Noogle Hall athletic and soccer teams. The sporting activities consumed much of my studying time.

The action I used to catch up in order not to jeopardize my academic career was ghosting.

The first year was fine academically. My grades could have been better; nevertheless, I was glad with the outcome of my effort. I decided after the first year to major in zoology, with botany as a minor. The second-year curriculum accounted for a third of the marks in the three-year BS honours degree. I was more interested in zoology than botany. My grades at the end of the second year were a reflection of that interest. I was fine going into the third and final year. I knew how much work I had to put in to get the grades I needed to qualify for graduate school. I wanted to apply for graduate studies in Upper Contica. My initial inquiries at Midway and Highland Universities in Grandonia and Amicus University in Multizone gave me a good idea of the grades I needed to qualify for admission.

My zoology grades were well within the ranges required by the graduate schools of all three universities. I had to work harder in botany. In addition to the three graduate schools abroad, I also hoped to gain admission to the MS program in the zoology department at the University of Nugget River. The new three-year honours degree required all students to select a course as an option for advanced studies.

I chose entomology. I also selected two courses in the department of botany. The bulk of my course work was in entomology, in the zoology department. I had developed an interest in insects at an early age in Natamia, my hometown in Nugget River. I accompanied our neighbours to their farm when I was 7 years old. The trip was my first time on a farm. I was eager to help them plant corn and root tuber. It was the season for those two crops, which were part of the staple diet in most West Gondwana countries. We had to plant the crops on four acres of arable land. After a preliminary period of their teaching me how to plant the crops, we started serious planting at about eight o'clock in the morning. We worked until the afternoon and took a short lunch break. When we resumed, we planted until sunset. I had not worked that hard until that day. I was exhausted and hungry at the end of the day.

Our neighbours had a mud hut on the farm. The thatched roof on the hut was cone-shaped, and the walls were circular. The hut was partitioned with specially woven raffia curtains into a kitchen and a section that was subdivided into a seating room and two bedrooms. The interior was well aerated at a constant, comfortable, cool temperature throughout the day. We had corn meal and fish stew for supper. The fish had been caught earlier in the day at a nearby river where we had a relaxing swim after our meal. I enjoyed the time we spent in the river, especially after a day of hard work. The river felt cold when I first stepped into it. The feeling was reminiscent of the cold morning showers at home on days when we ran out of charcoal and could not boil water. I took my first dive and held my breath for a few seconds. The brightness of the full moon illuminated the river that evening. I could see clearly all the way to the bottom of the river. I emerged expecting to admire the perfect symmetry of the round golden moon. Instead, I noticed that my view of the moon was cloudy. I wiped the water off my face and eyes for a better view. It was then that I discovered the cause of the cloudy appearance of the moon.

A dense, thick column of flying insects extended from the surface of the river into the sky. The column was more dispersed higher up in the sky. The haphazard flying motion of the insects was responsible for the obstruction of my view of the moon. The other members of our group in the river also saw the insects. My neighbour's husband told us he had observed the same phenomenon for the past couple years, at about the same month and hour of the day. For me, that view influenced my choice of a career later in life. I was curious enough to swim close to the area of emergence and trap a few of the insects. I discovered that the almost-blinding reflection of the moon on the surface of the river at the area of emergence was caused by thousands of bubbles from which the adult insects emerged. I was fascinated to watch the bubbles burst soon after arriving at the surface of the flowing water and deliver their cargo of adult insects. I watched the phenomenon for several minutes. I knew then that I wanted to learn more about insects, especially the insects I saw that night.

I realized the fulfillment of my childhood desire when I graduated in June 1976 with entomology as an option for advanced studies. My grades in all the entomology courses were above average. My best grade was in the course on aquatic invertebrates. It was fascinating to finally discover the mechanisms involved in the emergence of adult aquatic insects that use bubbles. I also learned that the insects I'd seen emerging as a little boy on my neighbour's farm could have been blackflies, mayflies or other aquatic insects. The bubbles that carried them to the surface of the river used a buoyancy mechanism and provided a dry environment for their wings. One of the papers I wrote as a project for my final examination dealt with the role of bubbles in aquatic insects. It was exciting to discover that bubbles played a role in respiration and were also used for pressure detection in some species of aquatic insects.

When I received the result of my BS honours examination, I sent letters of application to the three graduate schools I had corresponded with. I also asked the University of Nugget River to send my academic transcripts to the schools. Two of my professors in the zoology department and another in the botany department sent letters of recommendation to the three schools on my behalf. I had learned from the Multizonian and Grandonian embassies in Beaufort that it would take about a year to process my documents to send to the schools if my graduate school application was successful. The one-year waiting period fit well into my schedule.

National Service

Under the agreement signed by all first-year university students, we were required to do a year of national service after our graduation. Graduates were sent to different parts of the country to serve for one year with minimal pay in industry schools, hospitals and technical and vocational institutes. Three classmates and I were selected to do our national service as teaching and research assistants in the zoology department at the University of Nugget River. Being asked to stay in the department was a tentative confirmation that we were being considered for postgraduate studies.

The year of service in the department exposed us to various aspects of research and teaching. I learned a lot more about the department during my national service tenure. Academically, I developed a better appreciation for teaching and research work. I assisted the head of the department on a couple research projects. One of the projects kept me busy most weekends. I had to keep an all-night vigil once every month to observe the burrowing and mating behaviour of a laboratory colony of large, local, edible snails, *Achatina achatina* (Achatinidae). In the other project, I investigated the incidence of helminth parasites of the domestic chicken, *Gallus gallus domesticus*, and crows (Corvidae). The chickens were purchased from different locations in Eastern Nugget River, and crows *Corvus species* were hunted down from the same region. Both projects exposed me to the many frustrations and occasional accidental triumphs involved in scientific research. The most demanding aspects of my national service work were the preparation and supervision of laboratory classes. The research projects were more challenging mentally, but the laboratory supervision was tiresome. I was a laboratory demonstrator for first-year medical and zoology students. I worked in two three-hour laboratory sections weekly.

Socially, I spent most of my spare time with my two sisters and their boyfriends. I shared a house with my two sisters during the duration of my national service. We had parties and went out for dinner whenever it was feasible. I paid the occasional visit to my parents and the rest of the family in Aurus. My parents were aware of my plans to continue with my studies abroad. My dad was supportive. My mom was hesitant at first because she feared I might not come back to Gondwana. She later changed her mind but reminded me whenever we were alone never to forget my roots. Her fear was not without cause. One of her nephew's went to a Derkland university to study and ended up staying for 10 extra years. I have hitherto not forgotten my roots, but my mom's concern for my safety was a premonitory feeling of an event that occurred after I left Nugget River. I knew I had a good chance of being offered a scholarship for an MS program in entomology at the University of Nugget River after my national service tenure. I would have liked to continue with my budding entomology career at the University of Nugget River, but I felt I needed a change. I wanted to broaden my knowledge on insects. I knew that my chances of achieving my goal were better abroad because of the availability of modern research laboratories and research grants.

CHAPTER 2
Preparation for Journey to Multizone

A couple weeks after I was awarded the scholarship, the time and energy I'd invested in planning paid off. I submitted duplicate copies of my medical examinations to the Multizonian embassy a month after my award. While waiting to hear from the Multizonian immigration authorities, I wrote both the GRE and TOEFL papers six months before my date of departure. The results of both examinations were communicated to me three months after I wrote the papers. I did well in both examinations. Amicus University informed me they'd received my results from Neewton and had decided to exempt me from taking special English classes. The Multizonian embassy also informed me six months after I submitted my medicals that I had passed the medical examinations, and the results were acceptable to enable me to enter Multizone and proceed to study at Amicus University. They issued me a letter of medical clearance. I was further informed that copies of my medical examinations, together with x-ray films, were sent to Multizonian immigration in Looney Bay and to their West Gondwana regional archives in Elbony.

My preparation was on schedule as I had planned it until mid-August 1977, exactly a month before my date of departure, when I ran into a snag. I'd applied for a Nugget River passport in Beaufort at the time I submitted the results of my medical examinations to the Multizonian embassy. The passport office had informed me the passport would be issued when the Multizonian embassy approved my medical examination. I communicated the results of my medical examination to them the same day I heard from the Multizonian embassy. I also showed them proof of my scholarship for graduate studies at Amicus University. The passport was to be issued a week after I informed them of the results of my medical examination and showed them proof of my admission to Amicus University.

I received a call for an interview at the passport office after I made several calls and waited for two extra weeks after the scheduled one-week waiting period. I learned during the interview that my passport was ready, but I had to pay extra money to receive it. I knew immediately I was being asked to pay a bribe. My response, without hesitation, was no. It took patience and several calls and a visit to the passport office by the head of the scholarship secretariat for the passport to be released to me. Personally, I think it is shameful to have to pay a bribe to obtain a passport in one's own country. It is the right of citizens of civilized and democratic nations to receive such basic services without any restrictions or preconditions for personal gain by elected officials. I made arrangements for booster shots and various immunization vaccines after I received the passport.

I was able to get all my preparations done a couple weeks ahead of my departure date. The thought of leaving my two sisters alone in Nugget River scared me. I respected their independence as mature adults, but I worried about their safety after my departure. I also spent a great deal of time worrying about my flight to Multizone. It was going to be my first time on a plane. I am acrophobic. I could not imagine myself on an airplane at 30,000 feet above the ground, travelling at more than 500 miles per hour. My elder sister had flown several times. She did her best to calm my fears and anxiety. She told me what to expect and made me aware of the weightlessness I would experience when the plane ascended and descended. She also did her best to explain the motion of a plane if it encountered turbulent airflow. Her explanation made me more worried. My mom's asthma was another source of anxiety for me. She was fine and had not had another major asthma attack since the last episode. Her asthma responded well to treatment with corticosteroid inhalers whenever she had minor flare-ups. Her improvement abated my concern and fear that she might not survive one of the violent attacks.

I was not worried about my father. He was in good health. My parents were in their late fifties in 1977. My father looked younger than his age. His vigour was due mostly to his ability to maintain a healthy lifestyle after a serious illness in 1970. The doctors had told him to quit smoking to improve his chances of recuperating. His health had improved after he gave up smoking. He'd also taken to bike riding and walking daily. I spent a week with my parents in Aurus a month before my departure to Multizone.

I returned to Beaufort after the visit to make final preparations for my departure. My tickets were ready when I returned from Aurus. My parents and the rest of the family came from Aurus a week prior to my departure to see me off. We had a family party on the eve of my departure. Everybody had fun at the party. My mother once again reminded me that she was worried about my leaving home. My elder sister made my favourite meal of fried plantain and black-eyed bean stew for supper. My parents and sisters gave me several farewell gifts. We ended the evening with prayer. I knew then that we would not see each other after my departure for two or three years. I estimated it would take about that length of time to complete my MS degree. My flight was at eight o'clock the next evening. I stayed up after the family reunion for a final inspection of my luggage. I wanted to be sure I had all the important documents I had to take with me.

My passport, inoculation certificate, certificate of medical clearance, evidence of financial support to attend Amicus University and visa for a stopover at Citadel Airport in Big Park were in my carry-on luggage. I had two extra bags of books and clothing for the cargo compartment. After assuring myself that everything was in place, I withdrew to bed at about two o'clock in the morning.

My mother woke me up at nine o'clock. She informed me that my classmate Bob, with whom I was travelling, was waiting to see me. Bob and I had grown up in the same town and attended the same primary and middle schools. We'd taken the high school equivalent and advanced-level programs in the same town but in different schools. We'd entered the University of Nugget River in the same year. He had been awarded a scholarship for an MS degree in insect biochemistry at the University of Bridgetown in Multizone.

His mission on the morning of our departure was to finalize our arrangements for getting to the airport. We agreed to travel to the airport together to save money on taxi fare. We had prearranged to sit next to each other on the plane for moral support. It was also his first time on a plane. He confessed to me that he was also nervous about flying. The look on his face that morning gave away his nervous feeling. His usually relaxed face was tense, and his eyes appeared bulky and shiny. I was also nervous, but looking at him made me feel brave. I even had enough courage to attempt to calm him down and assure him we would be fine on the flight. He told me he'd been advised to get drunk before boarding the plane in order to fall asleep during the flight.

I knew that his parents would be at the airport, and I told him my parents were looking forward to seeing his parents. Our parents had not seen each other since my parents were illegally expelled from Nugget River in 1970. At about five o'clock, my sisters and brother decided they also wanted to be at the airport. The unexpected increase in the number of people necessitated a change in our plan to go to the airport in one taxi. Each family arranged their own transportation, and we agreed to meet at the airport at six o'clock.

The Journey to Multizone

Bob and I met on schedule at the check-in counter. He was dressed in a grey suit. He looked smart. I noticed that he had gone for a haircut sometime after our morning meeting. Unlike his nervous look earlier in the day, his expression was calm and relaxed. It did not take long for me to figure out the reason for Bob's relaxed demeanor. I smelled liquor on his breath. He told me to sneak to the bar for some drinks. Unfortunately for me, there was not enough time to indulge in a nerve-calming binge.

Bob's and my parents spent most of the time prior to our flight catching up on news from the past seven years. Bob and I had our luggage checked in after an hour of waiting in line. There were several flights that evening. A large number of flights caused several hours of delay at the customs and immigration sections. Our flight was delayed for almost a couple hours. Saying goodbye did not come easily. It was an emotional farewell. I saw tears in the eyes of my mother and sisters. My dad gave me a bear hug and whispered words of encouragement into my ears. My mom told me to write often, and she kissed me and repeated her familiar sentence: "Please do not forget your roots." We waved our last goodbyes just before I entered the plane.

The plane was a 727 en route to Big Park's Citadel International Airport via Longhorn International Airport. Bob sat in a seat in the middle aisle, and I sat next to him. At first, I noticed that the female flight attendants wore traditional dresses and capes made from a clothing material locally woven in Nugget River from specially dyed cotton. The final product was a mélange of colourful pieces that were intermingled and sewn together. I had expected to see the flight attendants in skirts and blouses like those of flight attendants depicted on the billboards at the entrance to the airport. The flight attendants had smiles on their faces. To me, the smiles were a welcome sight. The smiling faces were a sharp contrast to the look on my face—but not the look on Bob's. He smiled also. I wished I had taken his advice. My nervousness intensified during the demonstration of safety procedures on board the plane in the case of an emergency. I was quiet and wished everybody on board the plane would be quiet also. I was irritated by all the laughter and conversation going on around me. The moment I dreaded finally had arrived.

We were told to fasten our seat belts as the plane taxied down the runway. I felt cold sweat on my forehead and under my armpits. I reached out for Bob's hand, and we held on to each other tightly. Seconds later, we were airborne. I closed my eyes and broke out into a running cold sweat all over my body. My palms got wet; my shirt got wet—everything got wet. I thought I was going to pass out at one stage. I mustered up some courage and opened my eyes for a couple seconds. I was not happy with what I saw. We were still ascending, and the airplane was slightly angled on a horizontal plane. I opened my eyes again when the voice of one of the flight attendants came over the cockpit loudspeaker to announce that we had reached the cruising altitude of 33,000 feet. Shortly thereafter, flight attendants came into the cabin to make sure everybody was fine and to take orders for food and drinks. I had to break the deafening silence between Bob and me and ask if he wanted a drink. We had two beers each. I felt light-headed after the drinks. I loosened up a little and engaged in a short conversation with Bob. When we'd settled down, we engaged in more conversation.

We exchanged information about the universities we had been admitted to. He knew more about Amicus University than I did about the University of Bridgetown. Among students at the University of Nugget River, Amicus University was more popular than the University of Bridgetown. He had read about Amicus University when deciding which university to attend. We knew that both institutions had a lot to offer us in our individual fields.

We also talked about the terms of the awards given to us by the government of Nugget River. We were bonded to work for the government for five years with full pay after graduation. I was to work with the Kilan River Basin Research Authority in Cascade Falls. Bob had to return to the biochemistry department at Noogle. I had spent the long vacation at the end of my second year at Noogle, working as a research assistant at Cascade Falls. I'd worked with a team of entomologists and fisheries biologists who collected and keyed out fish and immature aquatic insects. I'd made the acquaintance of one of the directors at the research facility where I worked. He'd suggested I come work with them after earning my BS degree. He'd recommended me for the award when the scholarship secretariat contacted him.

After our conversation, I read a book for a while. My involvement in the story helped to further calm my nerves. I was relaxed after about an hour into our flight. We had a smooth flight except for the occasional feeling of weightlessness when the airplane either ascended or descended suddenly to avoid turbulent airflow.

We stopped over briefly at the airport in Longhorn. Bob slept most of the way until we arrived in Longhorn. I woke him up after we landed. We had an interesting conversation about flying. We agreed that flying was not as terrifying as we had dreaded. We also agreed we felt more secure while in our seats. The occasional visit to the bathroom was frightening at first, but with time, we got used to standing and walking on the plane. Bob laughed at me and teased me when he noticed how wet my shirt was. The takeoff from Longhorn Airport was not as terrifying as the initial takeoff in Nugget River. I had acquired some level of bravery, perhaps because I knew what to expect. When the airplane leveled at the designated travelling height, we had the last call for drinks. Bob and I did not have any more drinks that night. I fell asleep while reading my book. We arrived at Citadel Airport at dawn. Our flight to Luxville's Passion Flower International Airport was not until later in the day, at three o'clock.

We took a tour bus to see parts of Big Park. Overall, I thought the city looked beautiful and was well maintained. I was amazed at the abundance of luxury items, including cars, in Big Park. There were so many cars that I wondered if anyone rode on buses. It was the fall season in Big Park. A few trees had shed their leaves. The majority of the trees had autumn leaves. It was the first time I'd seen the beauty of nature expressed in such vivid and lively colours. My appreciation of fall from the movies and photographs I'd seen in Gondwana was heightened when I saw the real thing. Our tour bus went to several other scenic places. At the end of our tour, I had second thoughts about my decision to apply to a university in Multizone. I would not have minded attending university in Big Park.

We arrived back at Citadel Airport an hour before our scheduled departure to Multizone. The airport was huge compared to the Fly High International Airport in Nugget River. Bob and I decided to look around the airport after lunch. We had to be sure not to get lost. The airport was busy that afternoon. There were long lines of travellers waiting to go through customs. An equally long line of people waited to collect their luggage. We visited several shops. We had a drink at one of the bars and returned to our section of the airport minutes before our time of departure.

We went through the gate and waited in the customs and immigration section to have our passports stamped. After about 10 minutes, we were called to the customs office. Our passports were stamped after the immigration officers had proof we were foreign students en route to Multizone for graduate studies. At the customs section, the officers asked to search our carry-on luggage at the security gate. Bob and I did not expect what happened after we gave them our luggage.

One of the customs officers suspected I had drugs in our carry-on luggage. His suspicion was due to the bulge on both sides of my briefcase.

I explained to him that the bulge was foam cushion to protect delicate contents from being damaged if the briefcase ever got dropped. My older sister's boyfriend manufactured briefcases in his spare time after work. He'd given the briefcase to me as a parting gift. Within minutes of his suspicion, despite my explanation, the officer ordered me to be detained and called airport security. I was searched, and my briefcase was ripped apart. The search revealed nothing but foam cushion, as I had maintained all along. The security officers apologized for the inconvenience and told me I was free to go. I demanded they either compensate me for my damaged briefcase or give me another one. To my surprise and disappointment, they informed me I was not entitled to any compensation. I refused to leave their office until I was compensated. Bob later informed me that he was worried about me. He thought of calling the Nugget River embassy in Big Park but decided to wait until after we discussed it. Eventually, I left the office with the leather covering of my briefcase ripped off on both sides. I had to leave the office to avoid missing my flight to Multizone. I was surprised the security officers and customs officials had refused to compensate me. I was bitter about the incident and disappointed I could not do anything about the situation.

We left Citadel Airport on schedule on a Multizonian 727 airplane. The flight attendants were courteous and treated us well. I observed that the Multizonian 727 was more elegant. It had movies on board, and the cabin was better decorated. I listened to music for most of the first hour after we were airborne. We had light refreshments and snacks about 45 minutes into the flight. I had my first taste of Multizonian beer just before dinner. I had heard much about Multizonian and Grandonian beer at the University of Nugget River. I'd been told the alcohol content was 5 percent per volume. The alcohol content of beer in Nugget River and most of West Gondwana was about 12 percent per volume. I had worked in Nugget River with Grandonian volunteers who complained about the high alcohol content of the local beer.

I understood the complaint of the volunteers, whom I met in Nugget River after I had my first gulp. I liked the soft and pleasant taste and the lack of a potent smell of alcohol. I do not like drinking alcoholic beverages, but I enjoyed and savoured my first bottle of Multizonian beer. I paid the flight attendant with Derkland currency. She gave me my change in Multizonian currency and politely explained the exchange rate of both currencies to Bob and me. We told her that it was our first time abroad and that we were excited about going to study in Multizone. She spent most of her spare time talking to me.

She was interested in learning more about East Gondwana. I learned during our conversation that she planned to visit Stillsland as soon as she could afford the trip. She was eager to see the animals in East Gondwana, especially in the Green Park. "What are the animals in West Gondwana like?" she asked. I gave her a brief account of West Gondwanian animals, remembering to inform her of the paucity in the fauna compared to East Gondwana. I had spent a couple weeks at a game reserve in northern Nugget River in the final year of my BS program. The field trip was a part of the course on conservation and management of wildlife. The knowledge I'd accumulated on the field trip enabled me to pass valuable information to the flight attendant. I informed her of two female Multizonian tourists I'd met at the game reserve. They were from Lushberry. I'd made the acquaintance of the two ladies, and they'd spent a couple days on the Noogle campus as my guests on their way back to Multizone. I told the flight attendant I was looking forward to meeting the two female tourists again. We had maintained correspondence with each other, and they promised to visit me at Amicus University.

After 15 minutes of interesting conversation, the flight attendant wished me luck at Amicus University and went back to work. I read my book after dinner and fell asleep. A voice from the cabin speakers woke me, informing the passengers of our projected time of arrival at Passion Flower International Airport in Luxville. Bob and I ordered another round of drinks, and we toasted to successful careers at our universities in Multizone. We landed at about six-thirty local time. Bob's plane to Bridgetown was departing at seven o'clock; thus, we had no time to engage in further conversation. We hugged each other, said goodbye and promised to write and call as often as possible. I had no trouble making it through customs and immigration, except for spending a long time waiting in line. I showed the immigration authorities all the required documents, including my certificate of medical clearance, proof of admission to Amicus University and proof of financial support from the government of Nugget River. I discovered in the luggage section at customs that one of my bags was missing. The baggage department told me they would contact me if they found the bag. I was not happy about my missing bag. I thought Air Multizone should have taken better care of passengers' luggage. I had some priceless books and research materials in the lost bag.

I did not expect anyone from campus to meet me at the airport. Amicus University had resumed a week prior to my departure from Nugget River. My supervisor did not know my exact day of arrival. I'd sent him a telegram to let him know I would be a week late because of delays at the scholarship secretariat in making plans for my monthly stipends through the embassy of Nugget River in Looney Bay. I took the airport transit bus to Luxville. A friendly taxi driver drove me to Amicus University at nine o'clock on October 15, 1977.

CHAPTER 3
Amicus University in Luxville

Amicus University looked beautiful at night. After a couple fruitless attempts to locate the director of international student affairs, I ended up in one of the residences on campus. Officials at the residence told me I was on the wrong campus. I'd been admitted to the department of entomology at Sunnydale College, a campus of Amicus University. The Sunnydale campus was a 45-minute drive from the downtown campus. The residence manager gave me accommodation for the night and promised to help me get to Sunnydale College the next morning.

Morning arrived faster than I was used to. My internal clock was in total disarray after I had travelled across several time zones. My body yearned for more sleep, yet I could not afford extra sleep. The residence manager had arranged an eight-thirty ride for me to Sunnydale College. A worker in the residence was going to an airport close to the Sunnydale campus, and he agreed to give me a ride. He showed me the airport from which he was departing when he drove past it. I observed that Passion Flower International Airport was a more modern and bigger airport.

Sunnydale Campus

He dropped me off in front of the main residence at the Sunnydale campus and wished me luck. I took my luggage into the building and went to the reception desk, where I was informed that my supervisor had reserved a room for me. The receptionist gave me the keys to my room and duplicate registration forms. I was supposed to pay a damage deposit before my occupancy of the room. Unfortunately, I did not have enough money on hand. The receptionist agreed to hold on to an equivalent amount of the traveller's cheques I had on me until I could pay her.

My room was on the top floor of a five-story building. The view of part of the campus from my room was magnificent. It would have been great to see the whole campus from that height. A quick survey of my room revealed a double bed and an area for studying. The bookshelves in the study area were built into the wall, directly above a large oak table. The only other noticeable item in the room was an open closet in the wall at the foot of my bed. The bathrooms and kitchen were located down the corridor, in a separate area of the building. We had four bathrooms for 12 students. The kitchen was well equipped. I was told we had the option of either eating in the cafeteria or preparing our own meals.

After looking around the building, I went back to my room and unpacked some of my bags. I discovered that customs officials had looked through the bag I had in the luggage compartment. I noticed the items in the bag were rearranged. A lovely wooden Gondwanian carving given to me by my dad was damaged. I took out the carving and was relieved because the damage was fixable. I was unhappy about the chaotic rearrangement of my items. When I got tired from unpacking, I relaxed on my bed and spent some time in deep meditation. I thanked God for my safe arrival and asked for guidance and protection during my time on the Sunnydale campus.

After a relaxing, warm bath, I dropped off the application forms to the receptionist on my way to the department of entomology. I was lucky the residence was close to the entomology department. It was chilly, and I did not have the proper clothing for the cold fall weather.

The Department of Entomology (Sunnydale Campus)

The entomology department on the Sunnydale campus was located on the second floor of a building shared by other departments. Dr. Howard, my supervisor, was at a seminar when I arrived in the department. His secretary told me he had been expecting me. She asked if I wanted coffee, but I opted for tea. I drank little coffee when I first came to Multizone. She told me they thought I had given up on coming. They had not received the telegram I sent to inform them I would be a week late in arriving.

Dr. Howard came back to his office a few minutes before noon. I had just finished my first cup of tea when he walked in. The most noticeable thing about him was his accent. One could tell by listening to him that he was originally from Hyland. I apologized for arriving a week late. He told me I had not missed much because classes had started three days later than the college had planned. "The delay," he added, "was due mostly to late registration by new students." He noticed I was not properly dressed for the cold weather and promised to lend me some of his fall clothes until I purchased my own. I was a few inches taller than he was. I guessed I would fit into his clothes, albeit with some discomfort. I thanked him for his kindness.

Dr. Howard took me on a tour of the department. He introduced me to some of the staff who had not gone for lunch. I also met some of the graduate students. He showed me my space in the graduate students' laboratory. We ended the tour in his office. He promised to introduce me to the rest of the department the next day. Air Multizone called the entomology office while Dr. Howard and I were touring the department. They left a message with the secretary that my bag had been found and would be returned to me after supper. I called Air Multizone at Passion Flower Airport and gave them my residential address because the secretary and other staff in the entomology office would be gone by five o'clock in the afternoon. Dr. Howard apologized for not being able to take me to lunch that afternoon because he had a prior lunch appointment. We said goodbye, and I went to the cafeteria for lunch.

The cafeteria was packed with Sunnydale students and other students from a high school located on the Sunnydale campus. I waited in line for my turn and ordered a meat sandwich and orange juice. I enjoyed my lunch, but I wished I had some company. I was not used to eating alone. The atmosphere in the cafeteria was reminiscent of that at the University of Nugget River. Loud conversation and shouting were interspersed with the constant clinking of cutlery and plates. When I returned to my room after lunch, I noticed that my bed had been made.

I was also supplied with new sets of towels. I had a refreshing, long nap. I woke up in time to watch a magnificent sunset.

The beauty of the sunset was augmented by the brilliant fall colours of the vegetation, especially the leaves of the maple trees visible from my window. The leaves glowed and yielded their inner beauty when bathed in the piercing rays of the huge red sun. From a distance, the scenery captured my attention, and it was as if nature had presented me with a welcoming gift. There are moments in our lives when nature reveals her splendid beauty to us if we care to listen, watch, touch, smell or taste. I have lived spiritually on that scenery, and it has given me more appreciation and respect for the Creator. I get daily strength from that fleeting moment in October 1977, when I cared enough to watch. It taught me to see the beauty in all of God's creation. I will never forget that beautiful scenery as long as I exist. The sun finally disappeared from the horizon. The scene ended sooner than I would have liked. I closed my eyes for few seconds and gave thanks to God for the beautiful scenery.

A knock on my door interrupted my meditation. The gentleman I met at the door told me I had a phone call from Air Multizone. I rushed to the residential phone on the first floor, and Air Multizone told me my bag would be delivered at two o'clock the next afternoon instead of five o'clock that evening. The delay was because the director of Air Multizone's lost-and-found department at Passion Flower Airport was not available to sign the final document to release my bag. I was disappointed at the news. I went back to my room to finish unpacking my luggage. My family album caught my attention in the midst of my unpacking my bags.

My elder sister Georgina had given the photo album to me as a token of our promise to each other never to forget the family. It had been only three days since I left Nugget River, yet I already missed my family. For a moment, I wished I were back in Nugget River. I could not come to grips with the fact that I would not see my family again for the next three years. I looked through the photo album three times. I had different thoughts of what the future had in store for my family and me. I knew we would see each other again. I was consumed by the thought of our reunion. The growth and life experiences each of us would have gone through were prominent in my wandering mind. I mentally reassured myself that distance and the lack of physical contact were not strong enough to break the bonds of friendship and love that had developed among us.

I made the acquaintance of my neighbours later that evening. I also met Noah, a graduate student, that evening. He was from the Science University in Union City, Nugget River. He told me of three other Nugget River graduate students on the Sunnydale campus and promised to introduce me to them the next day. Noah and I spent most of the evening getting acquainted. He treated me to a special meal that he prepared. I learned from him that it was cheaper to cook than to eat in the cafeteria. We also discussed life on campus and in residence. I was more relaxed that evening and had a good sleep.

On my way out to the department the next morning, I picked up a note left in my pigeonhole mailbox by the receptionist. The note was from Air Multizone to confirm the delivery of my bag at two o'clock that afternoon. I met Dr. Howard in his office at nine forty-five, and we went for coffee together. Most of the staff and a few graduate students were at coffee that morning. My supervisor introduced me to the group. I had a good time with those who were present and promised to visit them in their offices and laboratories. I met the rest of the staff and graduate students after coffee. Among the 12 graduate students, five, including myself, were not Multizonian.

Kenny was from Naman, and he worked under the supervision of Dr. Howard. Jose, who also worked with Dr. Howard, was from Aldiva. He, his wife, and their five children became good friends of mine. I visited them often and enjoyed delicious enchiladas and tacos made by Gina, his wife. The other two foreign students were from the Seashell Land. My office space was next to Jose's in the graduate students' laboratory, and I got to learn much about his research work. He worked on the effect of low temperature on the survival of overwintering eggs of a forest insect. I stayed in the department until lunch break and then went to Noah's office in the agricultural engineering department.

We went to the cafeteria, where I met the other three graduate students from Nugget River. They were eager for news about Nugget River. All of them had relatives in Nugget River, and they were worried about their relatives' welfare. They wanted to know about the political and economic atmosphere in Nugget River. They were also interested in the military coup d'état that had overthrown the democratically elected government the year before I left Nugget River. We had a good lunch and exchanged addresses and phone numbers.

I went back to my room to wait for my bag from Air Multizone. The taxi that brought my lost bag was an hour late. The driver told me he'd gotten caught in heavy traffic between downtown Luxville and the airport near the Sunnydale campus. I was relieved to see my bag again. It had been banged around, and the lock on it was damaged. I had to force it open. Surprisingly, all my books and the other items in the bag were in good shape. I later learned the bag mistakenly had been placed on a flight to West Allemagnia at Citadel Airport in Big Park. After unpacking the bag, I called Dr. Howard and asked to take the afternoon off. I had gone to the bank and received cash for my traveller's cheques in order to buy warm clothes and pay my residential damage deposit. Dr. Howard had kept his promise and sent me some of his fall clothes earlier that morning. Contrary to my expectations, his clothes were too tight to make me comfortable; I was bigger than his size of clothes. The community of Delmount, where I went to do my shopping, was at the southwest end of the campus. Part of my route to the store was along the banks of the Port River across the street, which bordered the west side of the campus. I changed into my new fall clothes in the store after I purchased them. With my supervisor's clothes tucked away in my shopping bag, I decided on the way back to my residence to discover more about the scenery of Sunnydale College.

My discovery walk took me to the site where additional buildings on campus were under construction. It was a cold day. I wondered how the construction workers could endure the cold. My next stop was the outdoor sports arena, where I watched the practice routine of a soccer team. I ran into one of the graduate students from Nugget River, and he invited me to his house at the married students' residence on campus. I spent the rest of the afternoon at his house. I enjoyed playing with his 3-year-old son. His wife was glad to hear news about Nugget River. He invited me to stay for dinner, but I declined because I had a dinner appointment with Noah. After dinner, I went to the department to clean out my study desk, bookshelves and laboratory space. When I returned to my room, I wrote a letter to my family in Nugget River. Just before I withdrew to bed, one of my neighbours dropped by and offered to lend me extra blankets. I was grateful for his offer. The previous night had been chilly, and I'd been cold in bed. He explained to me when he came back with the blankets that heating for our rooms would not be operational until the end of October. I slept better that night.

I woke up the next morning with stiffness all over my body. I had not jogged for more than a week. I could tell my muscles were yearning for exercise. It is a wonder what the human body can become addicted to. Even exercise, if done on a regular basis, can become an addiction. To relieve the stiffness in my muscles and satisfy my craving for exercise, I went jogging that morning. I jogged several times around the football field without the appropriate jogging suit for the cold weather. I made it to the department on time after my exercises. Dr. Howard had left a note in my mailbox, inviting me to a social gathering at his home on Saturday evening. He offered to pick me up half an hour before the scheduled starting time of five o'clock. It was Thursday morning when I saw his note. He was not in the department that morning, and I guessed he'd left the note sometime on Wednesday. I completed a couple important tasks in the department that morning.

I went to the library, where I arranged for a familiarization tour and picked up my library card. When I was done in the library, Dr. Howard and I had a discussion on the courses I had to take in the first year of my program. We talked about possible research topics and plausible sources of obtaining funding for each topic. We also agreed to meet monthly to discuss my progress and other matters that might come up.

I attended my first class later that morning with Dr. Bright. He taught a course on how to give effective seminars. That particular course was mandatory for all first-year graduate students. I enjoyed the class and found most of the material he presented informative. By the end of the day, I'd met with all the professors in whose courses I had enrolled. The meetings had been arranged by the professors to discuss the materials the courses would cover. I had an equally productive Friday and received my first assignment from Dr. Bright.

The get-together at Dr. Howard's home was interesting and amusing.

Every graduate student and most of the staff were present. I used the opportunity to learn more about my colleagues and professors. I also spent time talking to Dr. Howard's family. His wife was completing her dentistry degree at the children's hospital in Luxville. Their two daughters, who were still living at home, asked a lot of questions about Gondwana. I had fun talking to them and correcting some of their misconstrued ideas about Gondwana. Except for the get-together at the Howards', the weekend went by rather quickly.

The volume of academic work increased with time, and I had little time to do other things. The weather also became unfriendly with time. It turned very cold about mid-November. My anxiety to see and touch snow increased with each passing day. I listened to the weather forecast eagerly and often. Finally, the radio announced on a Friday afternoon in the latter part of November that it was going to snow the next day. I was up early on the day snow was expected. I looked out my window and was disappointed there was no snow on the ground. At about three o'clock that afternoon, I went to the town of Delmount for my weekly grocery shopping. On my way back, I noticed some white substance falling. At first, I did not know it was snow. My idea of snow was totally different from what I saw. It did not feel heavy, contrary to what I'd anticipated. I caught a few of the white flakes, and then I heard a young girl some distance away shout, "Snow! Snow!" I couldn't believe my ears. I then realized the flaky white substance was snow. I stood for a while and watched the flakes fall from the sky. I was so absorbed in and excited about the scene that I momentarily forgot about the cold weather.

I finally saw and touched snow. That encounter will remain with me for as long as I live. I increased my walking pace. I couldn't wait to get home and get rid of my bags of groceries. I couldn't wait to get to my room and get my camera. The frequency and number of flakes increased with every step I took. By the time I got to the residence, there was a little accumulation on the ground. It was fun to walk on the snow, but it melted as fast as it accumulated.

I sat by my window after unloading my groceries. It was beautiful to watch the snowfall. Everything turned white in the distance. The only other colours visible were the fall colours of some leaves that interfered with the dominating white colour of the different shapes and sizes of falling snow. The scene was reminiscent of the emergence of the mayflies I'd witnessed as a young boy on my uncle's farm in Gondwana. It snowed intermittently until about six-thirty. I went outside after it stopped and noticed that contrary to my expectation, little snow had accumulated on the ground. I managed to collect some of the snow with both hands, squeeze it together and make a snowball about the size of my knuckle. It was fun to throw the snow. The fun was short-lived. The snow melted soon after the last downpour. I was happy I had fulfilled a childhood fantasy. I'd touched snow.

It snowed again the next morning. There was more snow than the previous day. I noticed on my way to church that despite the heavy snowfall, there again was little accumulation on the ground. Much of the snow melted because of the steady shower that lasted the rest of the day. The calming sound of the raindrops against the roof and windows of my room reminded me of the rainy season in the months of July, August and part of September in the Kilan region of Nugget River, where I'd grown up.

The skies cleared on Tuesday, and we had pleasant weather for the rest of that week. By the end of November, it had snowed quite a bit. There was an accumulation of close to six inches of snow on the ground. The nearby Port River was frozen enough by the end of December for people to cross-country ski and drive snowmobiles on it. Unfortunately, my meagre allowance prevented me from indulging in any winter sporting activity. The local skating arena became a favourite place of mine. I enjoyed watching people skate. I even had the opportunity to try on skates. The manager of the arena was kind and allowed me to use a pair of his skates without any charge.

My first encounter with skating was probably my last. After I got my skates on, I could barely move. All sorts of ideas went through my mind when motion became impossible. I tried to apply the theory of skating I'd learned in my advanced-level physics class in secondary school. The latter attempt produced some result, but within seconds, I was flat on my butt. After several failed attempts, I crawled to the side board and managed to get off the ice. I made a promise to myself after my poor performance to learn how to skate, but I never had time. A few days after my ignominious performance on skates, one of the boys on my floor invited me to a hockey game. He had an extra ticket for a game at the Luxville National Hockey League Arena. I had developed an interest in ice hockey by watching the game on television.

I was one of the regular spectators of hockey games on our floor. The speed and smoothness of the players' skating amazed me, and believe it or not, the hard hitting—but not fights—got my adrenalin flowing. We arrived at the arena in time to have a couple hot dogs each. The Luxville team was at home that evening to play a team from Grandonia. We took our seats and watched both teams. The arena was packed that evening. My friend informed me there was an ongoing rivalry between the two teams. The Luxville team was given a slight edge going into the game. I couldn't wait for the game to start. I'd promised myself a treat to a hockey game when I left Gondwana. *I guess this is it.* The game started on time.

The skating was fast, the talent on both sides was great and the hitting was paralyzing. It was an interesting game. The Luxville team won by a two-goal margin. I still do not know how it happened, but after that game, I became a fan of the Luxville team, maybe because the team was in Luxville or maybe because I know a good team when I see one. I have never regretted the decision to be a fan of the Luxville team. Luxville won the most-coveted cup in hockey that year and the year after. I attended a couple of the parades to celebrate the return of the cup to Luxville. Unfortunately, my first visit to the Luxville arena that winter was also my last one during my time at the Sunnydale campus. I would have loved to watch the Luxville hockey team as often as I could, but money became a crucial limiting factor. I watched most of their games on television. My first winter at the Sunnydale campus was a good one.

Overall, I had a good first year at the Sunnydale campus. I worked hard and received excellent grades in all my courses. I learned a lot of new things in entomology that year. I also concurrently earned a correspondence diploma in vector-borne disease control from Needlepoint, Jasper.

Curricula development, delivery of instructional material and the system of evaluation at the Sunnydale campus were excellent. Unlike the system at the University of Nugget River, the final examination was no longer the major determinant of the grade the student received.

The final grade in each course was based on the sum of grades from frequent tests, field trips, term papers and presentations. The frenzy of last-minute studying to obtain a good grade on the final and only examination was no longer the focus of taking courses. At Sunnydale, I was more relaxed with my academic work. Socially, I did my best to fit in, but sometimes, as painful as it may be, one cannot always do as the Romans do. I did most of my cultural adjustment that year. I strongly recommend it be made mandatory for foreign students to arrive at their host institutions a couple months before classes begin. The extra time should be used in an orientation program that teaches students about the cultural values of their host countries. The experience will help foreign students in acquiring the valuable skills needed to adjust to their host countries. The experience will also lessen the confusing and sometimes frustrating struggle to balance academic work and cultural adjustment. I suggest the commonly observed poor performance of most foreign students in the first semester or year is due to the culture shock they experience. Believe me, I experienced it.

After the initial shock, my course work progressed at an encouraging rate. I spent a good part of spring researching publications relevant to my research project. Dr. Howard and I had agreed on a project that dealt with the biology of a family of insects in apple orchards.

I spent the first summer collecting and identifying the insects in sprayed and unsprayed apple orchards. I worked on Miridae (Heteroptera), for those who are scientifically inclined and interested in knowing the name of the insects. I also studied the number of generations of various species per summer and the duration of each instar. I had productive summer and fall field seasons with my research project. I learned a lot about the role of insects in the dynamic ecosystem of apple orchards. I was happy with the results of my first fieldwork. Further analysis of my data gave me a better idea of the changes required in my methods. I also had a better idea of the intervals required between sampling. The most obvious result was that unsprayed orchards had more beneficial (predatory) species of mirids than sprayed orchards. I must also add that they had more arthropod pests.

My second year at the Sunnydale campus was better organized. I was more relaxed with my academic work. My course load was as heavy as in the first year, but I worked extra hours because of my research project. I had the opportunity to travel to the experimental research station in Richardson during my second winter field season. I went to the experimental station with Malthus, another of Dr. Howard's graduate students. Malthus worked on the population dynamics of the tarnished plant bug in apple orchards. Our visit lasted for a week. We met with other entomologists who worked in apple orchards and had an informative and productive visit. I learned about new methods and techniques of locating and incubating mirid eggs. The latter two techniques enabled me to have a successful winter season.

My research work led me to the late Dr. Godfather at the arthropod history and identification research station in Looney Bay. May he rest in peace. He was the mirid expert at the research station institute, and he confirmed the identification of my mirid collections. I visited him at the research station several times, and we became good friends. He had collected mirids extensively across Multizone, including in the remote northern regions. We arranged to meet during my second field season at the agricultural research station in Stonefield.

My second field season with Dr. Godfather was a rewarding one. Working with him enriched my knowledge and experience in the ecology of apple orchard pests. I learned more from him than from any textbook on the subject of mirids. The results of my summer field season were more informative on the impact of predatory and phytophagous mirids in apple orchards. I managed to save up some money, and with financial help from my elder sister Georgina, I bought a $750 used car. I needed the car to enhance my frequent trips to orchards in Kenneth and other collection sites in Stonefield.

I had a productive second winter season. I used most of my time to work on incubating and hatching mirid eggs. My feeding tests also went well. I used red mites to determine the predatory value of mirids in the sprayed and unsprayed orchards. I completed my course work in spring and met Dr. Godfather at Kenneth in June for my last field research. He left Kenneth in the last week of June for more fieldwork in Flatland and Mountain View. I worked at the Kenneth experimental station until mid-August.

CHAPTER 4

The University of Flatland, Dusty Rose

I was admitted to the provisional PhD program in entomology at the University of Flatland (U of F) in the fall of 1979. I initially heard about my supervisor, Dr. Turbulus, through Dr. Twistra, another member of the staff at the University of Flatland. Dr. Twistra was at the Sunnydale campus in January 1978 to deliver a seminar on the control of a group of medically important insects by sterile male release technique. He mentioned during the presentation that most of his fieldwork was done in East and West Gondwana.

It was a good and informative seminar. After the seminar, I introduced myself to Dr. Twistra and asked if I could come work in his laboratory after I completed my MS studies at Sunnydale. He told me he would have loved to have me in his laboratory if he had the grant to support me. He promised to discuss my interest in biting flies with Dr. Turbulus when he got back to Flatland. He also gave me Dr. Turbulus's address. I wrote to Dr. Turbulus soon after Dr. Twistra's departure from the Sunnydale campus.

In my letter, I told Dr. Turbulus about my interest in blackflies and my work on oviposition behaviour of a species of blackflies in Nugget River. He wrote back and asked me to send him my resumé and the transcripts of my studies at Noogle and the Sunnydale campus. I was excited and delighted on the day I received his letter informing me I could come to his laboratory for the PhD program. The formal letter of admission from the registrar's office contained further information on my grant and the requirements I had to satisfy to be awarded the degree. I was supposed to be in Flatland in October 1979, but I was delayed by my MS thesis. I worked on the thesis as hard as I could to submit it before leaving for the University of Flatland. I rushed to submit it, and I was therefore not surprised when the graduate faculty at Amicus University turned it down. The thesis was full of typing errors and a few inconsistencies. I resubmitted the thesis after three months and received a positive response the second time around.

The Department of Entomology (U of F)

Dr. Turbulus's family was helpful when I first arrived. I ended up spending the first couple weeks with his family. Dr. Turbulus's wife, Eva, and their two children, Susan and Peter, made me feel at home. Staying with his family helped break the ice, and we got to know more about each other. In retrospect, I wish I had not given him most of the information about me and my family in Gondwana.

After the initial familiarizing and honeymooning were over, I settled down to serious work. I was busy throughout the first half of the academic year. In addition to the time I spent to resubmit my MS thesis, I also had three full courses. The most challenging of my courses was advanced insect taxonomy. The course was taught by Dr. Hierarchus, who was the department chairperson when I arrived at the University of Flatland. The course dealt with the relationships and systematics of insects. The workload in that course was heavy. Every student in the department knew about that course and either hated it or dreaded having to take it. The assignments were numerous, lengthy and time-consuming. It took up to a couple weeks or sometimes a month to research and write up answers to some assignments. We usually received three assignments per week and were expected to hand the answers in the following week. Students had been known to take up to an extra year to complete and hand in their assignments. In the latter case, Dr. Hierarchus withheld the grades until the assignments were completed. He was a workaholic and expected students in the department to be the same. I'd learned about his strictness and high and unrealistic expectations of his students when I was at the Sunnydale campus. He expected students to be in the department on most weekends. I also knew he did not hold non-Caucasians, especially people from Gondwana, in high esteem. I experienced his latter attribute a month into his course.

He ridiculed me in the class by announcing that an article in the *Journal of Evolution* demonstrated, using molecular techniques, that natives of Gondwana were closer to apes than natives of areas with predominantly white populations were. I was speechless and surprised at the racially explicit nature and the timing of his comment. The lesson had nothing to do with human evolution. We were in the middle of a discussion on synonymy and how the rules of zoological nomenclature were applied to synonymous names. I was inexplicably calm. The ensuing silence was embarrassing. The comment took all the students by surprise. That was a warning I should not have neglected.

It turned out to be an almost deadly act of negligence. I stayed in the course and endured several more racially toned and demeaning comments. The most painful thing Dr. Hierarchus did to me was the grade he gave me at the end of the course. Despite his deliberate, unprovoked and constant referral to the inferiority of the natives of Gondwana, I kept my cool. I was one of the two students among five who completed and submitted all the assignments on time. To meet the deadline for submitting his assignments, I missed several nights of sleep and spent countless hours in the library, researching and working on the assignments.

Dr. Hierarchus gave me a six out of a maximum of nine. I knew I deserved better than a six. The wife of one of my colleagues sat in on the course and handed in less than a third of all the assignments a year after they were due. She received an eight from Dr. Hierarchus. She couldn't take what was going on, and she told me she knew she did not deserve the grade. She was shocked at the grade I received. Another colleague handed in his assignment after one year and received an eight.

Dr. Hierarchus's assault on me continued throughout my tenure in the entomology department at the University of Flatland. The most blatant attack came in my second year. Dr. Twistra gave a seminar on his sabbatical leave in Gondwana. In his closing remarks, Dr. Hierarchus looked in my direction and said, "The department is grateful Dr. Twistra made it back safely without ending up in a cooking pot." I stayed clear of him from that day on. It became difficult to interact with him. I stopped going to lunch to avoid further ridicule from Dr. Hierarchus. I resumed having lunch with the department when some of my colleagues insisted I come back. I had learned in my secondary school in Nugget River that only love conquers everything, even hate. Try as I did, it was impossible to avoid Dr. Hierarchus. I used to go to the department as early as seven o'clock in the morning. I'd discovered I functioned more effectively and could concentrate better academically in the early morning hours. I liked the fresh, cold breeze and the silence of the morning. Dr. Hierarchus was usually in at about the same time. I used to be worried, and his presence added to my anxiety. His antagonistic actions toward me succeeded in scaring me away from some social activities. I intentionally stayed away from parties I knew Dr. Hierarchus had been invited to. I also stayed away during coffee breaks. I could not shout or scream, "Racism!" for fear of being expelled from the department. There was no one to lodge a complaint with because Dr. Hierarchus was the chairman at that time. I kept as much within me as I could and prayed often, quietly, for patience.

Thank God I finished Dr. Hierarchus's course in January 1981. I also completed the other two courses I was taking. I still had not selected a research project by the summer of 1980. There were several projects I had considered and stored away in my file. Dr. Turbulus suggested some other projects. I also received several helpful suggestions from members of the aquatic discussion group of which I was a member. The group met once a week to discuss current topics and publications on the ecology of freshwater insects. Members of the group took turns discussing topics related to freshwater ecology that were closely related to their areas of research. I knew I would be working on some aspect of filter-feeding ecology of immature insects. The group was aware of my interest. A member of the group, Dr. Gilvester, informed me he had collected several taxa of filter-feeding insects from Bugg River in southern Dusty Rose. I discussed the information with Dr. Turbulus, and we agreed I should make an exploratory trip to Bugg River.

I made the trip in August 1980 with Eric, another graduate student who was working with Dr. Turbulus, on the formation and function of silk pads in immature blackflies. The trip was productive. We collected five different taxa of filter-feeding insects and brought live specimens back to the laboratory in Dusty Rose. I was not able to do much with the live specimens, but finding a good collecting site got me off to a good start. Dr. Turbulus arranged for me to spend the summer of 1981 at the agricultural research station in Hill Point.

I left for Hill Point in early spring for a couple reasons. I wanted to be at Bugg River soon after the ice broke to collect data on early instars of the two groups of filter feeders I had selected to study. I had most of the equipment I required. Some of my materials were still on order when I left Dusty Rose. I figured they would arrive in Hill Point by the time I needed them.

First Field Season in Hill Point

I had a productive summer. My experiments went well, except for the occasional problem with equipment and techniques. I was particularly happy with my laboratory feeding tests. I stayed at the community college in Hill Point and camped occasionally at a park through which Bugg River ran. Proximity to Bugg River enabled me to spend more time collecting from the river.

I made the acquaintance of the chief park warden, Edward. He was friendly and co-operative. His only objection to fieldwork was that I should not collect specimens in the park. I needed a permit to collect from the park. I did most of my collecting in parts of the river far removed from the park. I was allowed to stay in the park for two weeks at a time, and then I took a day off and came back. I fell in love with the park. The name of the park was derived from the images and drawings on rocks along the banks of the river. The art was the work of ancient tribes who'd once lived in that area.

The drawings told stories of the way things used to be. They depicted the days when man lived in harmony with nature and was a true custodian of that which God put him in charge of. I think we can learn a lot about preserving and respecting the environment from ancient tribes if we care enough and dare ourselves to respect their cultures. Touching the drawings on the stones made me feel, in an inexplicable way, connected to the past. In addition to the drawings, the park was also littered with hoodoos formed by the eroding actions of rain and wind. The perfect symmetry of some of the structures was suggestive of an unseen hand at work. Bugg River was like an oasis in the dry landscape. The banks were lined with trees and shrubs.

The river's name was derived from the cloudy appearance of the water. The river flowed through a sediment rich in deposits of calcium carbonate. The load of chalk as a result of erosion gave the water a cloudy appearance. The scenery was reminiscent of the biblical land of milk and honey mentioned in the Old Testament book of Exodus. The blueness of the distant mountains in Skyview broke the monotony of the grassy vegetation. The wardens arranged tours of the park for visitors. I took time off from my research and went on one of the tours.

The tours took visitors through some of the most scenic and pristine parts of the park. We also saw several diamondback rattlesnakes, white-tailed deer and countless numbers of gophers. We learned from our tour guide that buffalo used to roam the park long ago. We visited a cliff used by the ancient dwellers to hunt buffalo. The dwellers had chased the buffalo and forced them to fall off the cliff. We also had the opportunity to hunt for dinosaur fossils. The whole of southern Flatland, especially the Rivercamp area, had rich deposits of dinosaur fossils. Unfortunately for us, we found no fossils. We might have been either careless or simply unlucky in our hunt. Fossilized dinosaur eggs were found five years after our tour along the banks of Bugg River in the park.

My research work at the agricultural research station in Hill Point ended at the end of August. I returned to the University of Flatland at the end of the first week of September. I spent the week after I left Hill Point collecting immature blackflies from streams and rivers in southern and central Flatland. The latter collections were for a project: a new taxonomic key for the blackflies of Flatland. The project included Dr. Turbulus; Eric; Kevin, another graduate student of Dr. Turbulus; and me. The project was funded by the Department of Environment in Flatland. Dr. Turbulus served as an adviser. Kevin was the project leader. When I arrived in Dusty Rose, it took time for me to get used to life at the University of Flatland.

I was used to the soothing and calming music of birds and insects. I missed the natural and exquisite scenery of the park in Hill Point.

Getting back into the rustling routine of life on campus was not easy. I was the teaching assistant for Dr. Turbulus's agricultural entomology course. He gave me the laboratory and course contents soon after I returned from Hill Point. The materials for the course kept me busy and helped me get back into the routine of academic activity. I guess I needed a break from my research. My job as a teaching assistant kept me busy. My course load was not as heavy as when I first arrived in the department. I took a course on insect ecology in the department and audited another in the department of mechanical engineering. An aspect of my research required I have knowledge of some principles and experimental techniques of mechanical engineering. I had decided on a research topic that involved using two groups of filter-feeding insects to test the applicability of aerosol models of filtration in aquatic environments. The idea of testing aerosol models on biological filters had been suggested in a paper published in 1977 by two professors, Rubenstein and Koehl, at the University of California in Berkley.

I devoted most of my weekends and evenings to analyzing the data I'd brought back from my summer research at Hill Point. I also spent a lot of time developing a new technique for recovering polystyrene particles from the guts of the two species of immature insects I had selected to test the aerosol filtration models. I'd fed the particles to the insects as part of my experiments during the summer. My objective was to determine the various sizes and the numbers of each size of particles consumed by the immature insects. I ran into some problems with my techniques on particle recovery from the guts of the insects early in the process. A lack of time forced me to put the research work aside. I concentrated instead on a course in forest insect ecology and worked as a teaching assistant in the agricultural entomology course Dr. Turbulus taught. I enjoyed teaching the laboratory class for the agricultural entomology course. I had a good first week with the students. The second week proved to be even more enjoyable. I will always remember that second week because it was the week I met Luba, who is now my wife.

We met on a Friday afternoon, on September 18, 1981. I completed my laboratory class at five o'clock after the usual three-hour section. I was tired at the end of the section, but I was also happy with the performance of the students. It was stimulating to spend time with a group of students who were eager to learn.

I decided to stop over in one of the bars on campus for a soda. I ran into Diego on my way to the bar. I had met Diego in Hill Point during the summer, and we'd become good friends. Diego was a student in the department of mechanical engineering at the University of Flatland. We talked about the good times we'd had together in Hill Point during the summer. His sister had a summer job with one of the scientists at the experimental station in Hill Point. She and I had lunch together once. She was a medical student at the University of Flatland. Diego decided to accompany me to the bar to continue our conversation. On our way to the bar, we talked about the many new faces on campus. It was the beginning of a new academic year, and there were many undergraduate, graduate and transfer students on campus. We knew that most of the bars on campus were usually packed to capacity by six o'clock on Fridays, so we decided to hurry to get to the bar. We increased our walking pace, and just as we turned the last corner before the bar, we ran into a couple ladies.

Diego and I recognized one of them and stopped. I said, "Lilly, I have not seen you around lately." I had met Lilly and her boyfriend at a social gathering on campus. The other lady's face caught my attention. We looked each other in the eyes, and I felt as if I had just been struck by lightning. Her piercing bright green eyes made my heart race faster. She looked beautiful, and her blue dress revealed a slim and well-contoured body. I was dumbfounded and could barely speak a word. Lilly broke the silence by introducing her to Diego and me. I learned that her name was Luba. The four of us engaged in conversation for about 15 minutes. I mustered up enough courage to ask Luba for her phone number. She was hesitant, and I suggested I could meet her for coffee on Monday at the students' housing complex on campus. She did not give me a direct answer. She told me she usually stopped by the coffee shop in the housing complex briefly at ten o'clock on weekday mornings.

The weekend prior to our unplanned coffee meeting was a long one for me. I could hardly control my anxiety and desire to see Luba again. The image of her green eyes and the echo of her soft voice kept me from concentrating on my research and other academic work. I stayed up most of the weekend. It appeared to me the hours did not pass quickly enough. Time seemed, in my mind, to have slowed down. I glanced at my watch repeatedly and drank too many cups of coffee to count. I survived that tortuous weekend. I went to the coffee shop at the housing complex at nine-thirty on Monday.

She was 20 minutes late in coming to the coffee shop. Those 20 minutes were like an hour to my rugged and tired mind. In the interim, I thought she either had forgotten about stopping by the coffee shop or was busy with other things. The thought of not seeing her that day bothered me. I took sips of my coffee and consoled myself that she had not made any promises and that it was not a date. I was almost done with my cup of coffee, when she came into the coffee shop. I saw her and went to her. "I thought you were not going to come," I said in a shaky voice. She smiled and told me she'd been busy with an assignment for a paper. I offered to buy her coffee. We had a productive conversation about several topics. We discovered a lot about each other and agreed to meet at the coffee shop again the following day. We eventually started dating and became lovers.

Luba was studying for a bachelor of education program at the University of Flatland. She was friendly, and most of my colleagues and professors readily accepted her into the social circles in the entomology department. She was present at most of our departmental seminars. I accompanied her to some of the seminars in her department. Our proximity to each other's departments made it possible for us to see each other frequently. We became passionate lovers and good friends.

With Luba's help, I was able to refine and complete the analysis of my previous summer's data. I'd found out after the previous field season that I would need assistance for the next spring and summer field seasons. I had discussed the need for a summer assistant with Dr. Turbulus when I returned from Hill Point in August 1981. We'd agreed I should hire a student for the 1982 field season. When he learned I had decided to hire Luba, he was not in agreement with my choice. His main objection was that Luba and I were dating. I assured him Luba and I were mature enough to separate pleasure from work. I mentioned to him that Luba was the most qualified person for the assistance I needed. He agreed Luba was qualified for the job, but he still had reservations. I insisted on hiring Luba rather than spending time on training another student. I also knew Luba had done a lot of work on my research and could be trusted with the safety of my data. Dr. Turbulus finally agreed to let Luba be my summer assistant. Luba and I were glad he gave us the go-ahead.

I was surprised Dr. Turbulus agreed to pay her only $1,000. He informed me that his funds were running out. I believed his story, but I later discovered he had agreed to pay $2,500 to the summer assistant of another graduate student. Luba and I were not happy when we found out Dr. Turbulus was being unfair and untruthful to us. After careful thought, because we wanted to work together, we agreed on the amount. I suspected Dr. Turbulus's action was perhaps because he was not happy about Luba's and my working together. I convinced myself he would discard his doubt about my research getting done when I returned from the summer field season with good data. However, I soon discovered Dr. Turbulus had other motives for his preferential treatment of the summer assistant of the other graduate student. It became obvious that Dr. Turbulus's attitude and behaviour toward me had changed after my seminar on the status of my research.

I received negative and mostly non-constructive comments from him about my presentation. The comments were the first hint that something had gone wrong with our mentor-student, relationship. Some of the comments were personal in nature. My academic qualification and my suitability for the doctoral program were questioned. Dr. Hierarchus went as far as to ridicule my understanding of the theory of evolution. I made several attempts to try to find out the cause of Dr. Turbulus's sudden change in attitude toward me, but he barely gave me time to talk to him. I was not surprised at Dr. Hierarchus's behaviour. I had learned to expect such comments from him.

Luba was not happy with the comments either. She was at the seminar and thought I gave a good presentation. Three other professors from the department of zoology told me they'd enjoyed my presentation. I had insight into the objective Dr. Turbulus was trying to achieve.

A Salubatan student and I were at the Sunnydale campus together from 1977 to 1979. He came to the entomology department in Dusty Rose in 1981 for MS studies on genetic control of a medically important insect. The student was constantly told he was not good enough for the program. He did not complete his graduate program. He left due to problems with his grades that were beyond his control.

He enrolled in Dr. Turbulus's agricultural entomology course. He was ill before the midterm examination in the course. He requested and was granted permission to defer writing the midterm examination until the end of the semester. He and I were in shock when we learned of his expulsion from the department. He'd been given a failing grade for the midterm examination he had not written.

The unjustified expulsion of the Salubatan student taught me to watch out and concentrate on my studies. I knew after Dr. Turbulus's change in attitude that attempts would be made to expel me from the department. I knew my academic ability and performance offered him nothing to use against me. I guarded against being given the same treatment.

Second Field Season in Hill Point with Luba

Luba and I decided to leave for Hill Point early in spring because we wanted to get away from the department. We did not want to give Dr. Turbulus, Dr. Hierarchus or Dr. Twistra any chance to fabricate a scheme to expel me. We left Dusty Rose for Hill Point at the end of April. Dr. Turbulus gave Luba $500 of her summer salary and promised to pay her the remaining $500 at the end of the summer. We stayed with one of the technicians who worked in the entomology division at the research station. I wanted to be close to the research station for quick access to my experiments. I'd learned after the previous summer that I needed to be close to the research station. I had live insect specimens in a flow tank, and it was necessary to visit the laboratory frequently to feed them.

Our first week at Hill Point was nothing like my first week during the previous summer. I knew there was going to be trouble soon after we arrived at the research station. Some of the scientists and technicians with whom I'd become acquainted the previous summer treated me as if they never knew me. The worst treatment was being denied access to adequate laboratory space. I was also denied some of the other privileges I had enjoyed the previous summer. I complained to the section head, and he told me that space and funds were limited and that I should make do with what I was given. He'd known in advance that I was coming to spend the summer at the research station with Luba, yet he had not informed me of the shortage of funds and laboratory space. At the end of the second week at the research station, I decided Luba and I had taken enough rude treatment. We left the research station.

During that two-week period of rude and unprofessional treatment, my flow tank of live insects was tampered with on several occasions. The motor was shut off on a number of occasions. I managed, on occasion, to restart the motor. I had to make the long trip to Bugg River to replace my insects a couple times. The immature blackflies and mayflies died from asphyxia on those two occasions. I finally figured out that my tank was being intentionally turned off.

On one occasion, someone threw a biological insecticide, *Bacillus thuringiensis israelensis* (*Bti*), into the flow tank. I lost all my blackfly larvae, and the mayfly nymphs were adversely affected and had to be destroyed. I knew the insects died from the effect of *Bti* because of the telltale signature left behind by the mode of action of the insecticide. Blackfly larvae that had been killed by *Bti* usually remained in their attached positions at death and gradually decomposed. I had positive identification of *Bti* from water samples in the flow tank. The latter incident contributed to our decision to leave the research station and camp at Bugg River. I found out later that the cause of my problems originated from Dr. Turbulus. I was surprised my own supervisor could do such a thing to me. At least I knew why I was denied access to sensitive areas at the research station and why I was not given adequate laboratory space.

After we departed from the research station, Luba and I did not return to Dusty Rose immediately. We collected immature blackfly larvae from various locations in southern Flatland for the project on writing a new taxonomic key for the blackflies of Flatland. Upon our arrival in Dusty Rose, I observed that Dr. Turbulus was not surprised to see us back early. I told him about the problems we'd encountered at the research station and informed him I was going to complete the summer at Bugg River. He approved the decision to relocate to Bugg River but added that he doubted if there were accommodations and equipment for me to do a good job at Bugg River. I told him I was just doing my feeding tests and would do most of my analysis and other laboratory work when I got back to Dusty Rose. Luba and I stayed in Dusty Rose for a week. We had no place to stay, and we ended up spending the nights in my laboratory on campus.

Luba's twin sister, Lena, came with us on our return trip to Hill Point. She requested to join us for the summer in southern Flatland. She was having personal problems and needed space and time to work out her problems. We were fortunate she came with her van. We had planned on renting an apartment and turning a section of the apartment into a laboratory. Lena's van served a dual purpose. There was enough space in the van for my flume, and it substantially reduced the amount of travelling to Bugg River for my insects. We had succeeded in arranging to get distilled water and other essential equipment from the University of Hill Point.

We abandoned the plan to stay in the town of Bugg River when I received permission from the chief game warden, Edward, to use electrical outlets at the park. Luba and Lena made trips to the University of Hill Point to collect distilled water and ice for my feeding tests. The new arrangement turned out to be better than working at the research station. I no longer needed to maintain a supply of live specimens. I collected immature insects from a section of Bugg River a few kilometres from the park, starved them overnight in my experimental flow tank and ran my feeding tests the following morning.

We were allowed to camp in the park for 10 days at a time. We moved out at the end of the 10th day and came back after a couple days. I was lucky I'd met Edward. My research would have been seriously jeopardized without Edward's kindness. The memory of sharing my second summer with Luba and Lena at the park still lingers on. It was refreshing to sit around the fire at night after a hard day's work and listen to the calming sound of flowing water in the Bugg River. We also had a fantastic view of the northern lights, or aurora borealis, on most nights. In addition to having a productive and rewarding field season, we also became good friends with the wardens and went on a number of tours of the park with them. My feeding tests went so well that we finished a week ahead of schedule.

It was difficult for us to say goodbye to the wardens. It was even more difficult to leave the park. That summer was my last field season, and I knew it would be a long time before I saw the park again. During our last week in southern Flatland, we visited the Japanese Garden in Hill Point. The time we took off from my research work refreshed us before we returned to the University of Flatland. We collected blackfly larvae from several rivers on our journey back to Dusty Rose.

We arrived in the department to a rude welcome. I delivered my collections of immature blackflies to Dr. Turbulus. He took the collections from me and told me he wanted to discuss the problems we'd encountered at the research station with me the next day.

We were unable to get an apartment in Dusty Rose due mainly to the lack of money. Most of the landlords and management agencies wanted a damage deposit equivalent to a month's rent. All my attempts to get Dr. Turbulus to pay Luba the remaining $500 of her salary were unsuccessful. He promised to pay her the rest of her salary when we returned to Dusty Rose. Luba and I planned on using the money to pay the damage deposit required to rent an apartment. We ended up spending the night in one of the classrooms in the entomology department.

My meeting with Dr. Turbulus took place in his office after the ten o'clock coffee break. I suspected at coffee time that our discussion was not going to be pleasant. None of the people who came for coffee that morning showed interest in my story about the park during the summer. The atmosphere was unusual and tense. I felt as if I was among strangers. I had an ominous feeling that something bad was about to happen to me. I could hardly wait to get to Dr. Turbulus's office to find out what was going on.

The meeting was not a discussion, as I had hoped and anticipated. Dr. Turbulus ended up giving me a lecture on a letter he'd received from the Hill Point research station. I waited patiently and listened to everything he had to say. The letter alleged that Luba and I had been disrespectful to everybody at the research station. We allegedly had left the research station because we isolated ourselves and did not get along with people. He showed me the invoice of equipment and items I'd purchased from the supply store at the station. The invoice showed I had xeroxed $150 worth of materials and bought one gross of microscope slides. In conclusion, Dr. Turbulus told me that because I'd mismanaged my research grant and because of my behaviour at the research station, he was suspending my research work. He gave me one month to write up my thesis. He also took me off his budget until after I submitted the thesis to him. I told him that every allegation of rudeness and the items on the invoice were false. I reminded him of the trip Luba and I had made to Dusty Rose to inform him of the problems we had encountered at the research station. I also demanded to look at the invoice. He showed me the invoice, and to my surprise, I noticed that my signature on the invoice was forged. I'd signed an invoice before I left the research station for the park. The invoice I'd signed did not contain the purchase of microscope slides or $150 worth of xeroxing. I certainly would not have signed it, because Luba and I did not xerox $150 worth of materials or purchase one gross of microscope slides. I did not require microscope slides for any aspect of my research. I informed him about the forged signature and told him the invoice he showed me was not the one I'd signed before I left the research station. I reminded him that none of my experimental techniques required using microscope slides. Fortunately, Luba and I kept a record of all the xeroxing we did. I produced the record. All the xeroxing we'd done totalled forty-two dollars and some cents. He promised to investigate the forged signature and the validity of other items on the invoice and get back to me.

In the interim, I was still to write up my research, and there would be no funds for me until I handed in the thesis. He refused to delay the write-up and put me back on his budget until after his investigation of the allegations against Luba and me. When I asked him for the rest of Luba's salary, he told me that the balance would be paid after I handed in the thesis. I made several attempts to convince him that Luba and I needed the $500 to be able to rent an apartment. He disregarded my pleas for the money. I asked for a copy of the letter that accompanied the invoice. Dr. Turbulus promised to give me a xeroxed copy later. Before I left his office, he informed me that I was no longer part of the project on writing a new taxonomic key for the blackflies of Flatland. He said I needed time to write my thesis. He resisted all my efforts to work on the project. I had invested a lot of time and work into collecting blackflies all over southern Flatland for the project. I had also spent countless hours in the library, searching for literature relevant to the project. To further intimidate me, he repeatedly told me I would be expelled from the department if all five members of my dissertation committee did not accept the thesis, which was due in a month.

I left his office dejected, disappointed and angry. I knew I did not have much time, but I was determined to do my best. The only major hurdle was finding an apartment. Luba and I did not have enough money, and each day without an apartment brought me closer to doom. I knew I was out if I did not submit the thesis in one month. Luba and I almost panicked, but our undaunted efforts paid off after one week. We slept in a classroom and in my laboratory for that week. I had three weeks, and I knew I would need every minute of those three weeks. I also had two full loads of courses to complete. One of the courses was insect biochemistry with Dr. Twistra. The other was in the department of zoology. Dr. Twistra, either by design or accident, was the acting chairman when Dr. Turbulus intensified his efforts to disrupt my research project. The insect biochemistry course was demanding, and Dr. Twistra was not helpful. I had my share of Dr. Twistra's negative and racially toned comments. I endured his onslaught and completed the course. The grade he gave me revealed something important about grade fabrication in the department.

I received a passing grade, but it was below the class average. I became suspicious of the way grades were awarded in the department. I went back to my transcripts and discovered the same pattern of grade fabrication by professors in the entomology department. I'd received passing but below-class-average grades in all the courses I'd taken in the department. The discovery came as a shock to me, but I knew that protesting would cost me my degree. I had to dig deep to maintain my sanity and my interest in the program. My grades were not a reflection of my performance at the University of Flatland. My transcript from the University of Flatland was representative of fabricated rather than earned grades.

In the interim, Luba and I resorted to a nocturnal lifestyle to meet the deadline for the write-up. I would forever remain grateful to Luba for the countless hours she spent in the library. She became my third and fourth arms and eyes and second brain. It would have been next to impossible to meet the deadline without Luba. She typed up each chapter after I finished writing it. I submitted the thesis on time using the data from my first summer at Hill Point. I included a chapter on what needed to be done to make the thesis more complete. Dr. Turbulus was surprised I'd met the deadline. I could tell he was not happy about it. I waited for a couple weeks to hear from the supervisory committee. I did not expect any problem with the write-up, and I did not get one.

Dr. Turbulus reluctantly allowed me to continue with my research, but the rest of Luba's salary remained unpaid. Luba and I had borrowed money from a friend with the hope of paying her back when Dr. Turbulus paid Luba the rest of her salary. She never saw the remaining $500. I also never heard anything about Dr. Turbulus's investigation of the invoice and the accompanying letter sent to him from Hill Point. He also did not give me a xeroxed copy of the letter. I asked him for the investigative report and letter a number of times but received no answer from him. I knew I had to be careful not to annoy him by asking for the report and letter. He had his gun cocked and was just waiting for a chance to pull the trigger, figuratively speaking. The thesis write-up had been his best chance yet, and I knew he was not done.

Luba, however, persisted to demand what rightfully belonged to her. Instead of paying Luba the balance of her salary, Dr. Turbulus resorted to legality. He denied ever promising to pay her $1,000 and asked Luba to produce the letter in which he'd made the promise. Luba made it clear to him that the agreement on the salary had been a verbal one. She reminded him that the $500 she'd received from him was understood to be partial payment of her salary. Luba and I were surprised by Dr. Turbulus's denial. We had incurred a $500 loan due to his lie. Paying back the loan became a problem. Fortunately, our friend understood our predicament and gave us more time to pay her back. My suspicion that I was dealing with an unreliable and possibly psychopathic supervisor was strengthened by Dr. Turbulus's behaviour.

I doubled my efforts to finish my research. I knew I had to work harder and try to leave the entomology department as soon as possible. With Luba's help, I was able to process data from my second field season in time. In addition to a couple courses, I also successfully completed the foreign language proficiency examination required from all PhD students. I opted for the French language test.

With the course and language requirements behind me, I concentrated on the last part of my research work. I built scaled-up physical models of the filtering structures of the two immature insects I was studying. I used the models to elucidate the mechanisms used to intercept food particles from moving water (flow). The last part of the research kept me busy during the fall and winter of 1982. I towed the models through canola oil at different velocities, and I made a video recording of the towing experiments. The tapes provided useful information and revealed the relevant mechanisms used by each insect.

Throughout the latter series of experiments, Dr. Turbulus maintained his antagonism toward me. One of the tapes disappeared immediately after I completed my experiments. The tape was later found, but several important sections were erased from it. I found out from one of the technicians at the television studio where I'd borrowed equipment for my recording that Dr. Turbulus had taken the tape from their laboratory for editing. The laboratory personnel had allowed him to take the tape since he was my supervisor. I later discovered that the tape submitted with copies of my dissertation was not the copy I'd recorded from my experiments. In comparison to my tapes, the tapes that accompanied the dissertation did not include my image in the video as I stirred up the microbeads at the start of each new velocity of flow. The audio comments I'd made about flow patterns were also missing. The video appeared grainy and was poorly recorded under low-light conditions. Several other events in the entomology department were aimed at sabotaging my research work. A notable occurrence was the strange and inexplicable loss of valuable data after I stored them on computer. I almost lost all my files at one stage when I was writing the final draft of my thesis. Through it all, with Luba's encouragement, I was able to maintain a firm and positive attitude. I concentrated on my research work and absorbed all the shots that were fired at me. I almost lost my patience on a number of occasions, but I knew that would be counterproductive. I had become numb to derision and other things Dr. Turbulus was using to distract and derail me from completing my thesis.

The behaviour of Dr. Turbulus and some other professors in the entomology department at the University of Flatland defiled all the values my parents and other mentors had taught me. I'd been taught and encouraged to appreciate a good and productive student. Until I went to the University of Flatland, the professors who trained me had encouraged me to pursue my goals and strive to be productive. I had also learned to accept failure and use the experience to dig deeper for success.

My experience of hatred in the department of entomology at the University of Flatland exposed me to another facet of life. As painful as it was, I learned there are mentors who will hate you for working hard. The reason behind Dr. Turbulus's behaviour became clearer and clearer to me with time. When the harassment became unbearable, I took most of my work home and spent less time in the department.

Marriage

One bright spot during my ordeal at the hands of Dr. Turbulus was my relationship with Luba. Our friendship and honesty with each other stood the test of the harassment. We got married on December 18, 1982. The wedding took place in our apartment. Luba looked so radiant on our special day that she took my breath and heart away. It was a day to behold. We had a few friends over for the ceremony. I invited Dr. Turbulus, but he declined my invitation. Luba was reluctant to tell her parents because she was afraid of their reaction, especially her father's. He wanted his daughters to marry men from his homeland in the diaspora. Luba's twin sister, Lena, was Luba's maid of honour. My best man was Dr. Femi, a doctor from Kolaland. He was a good friend of mine. He was an intern at the Cancer Institute in Dusty Rose. We spent the evening of our wedding day at Dr. Turbulus's Christmas party. We received a pair of red-hot underwear as a wedding gift from the professors and graduate students. It is an understatement to describe the underwear as being suggestive. Luba and I were momentarily taken aback when we saw the pair of underwear. We burst into laughter, and then everybody at the party joined the chorus of uncontrollable laughter. I was speechless except to jokingly say, "You are all perverts disguised as entomologists." Of course, I could hardly wait to see Luba in her underwear.

We had a good time at the party and enjoyed all the entomological humor. Luba made everybody laugh when she quipped, "Entomologists are like insect pests that have developed resistance. You can spray them, and they still come back." We wanted to leave the party early and go dancing, but my bad right knee prevented us from going out.

CHAPTER 5
Knee Surgery

I had injured my knee in Nugget River during a high school soccer game. The doctors in Nugget River told me the injury was minor. They advised I rest the knee and give it time to heal. I was able to play soccer again at the University of Nugget River after several years of avoiding contact sports. I also played inter-squad soccer at the Sunnydale campus of Amicus University. I reinjured the knee a couple months before my marriage while playing Ping-Pong in October 1982. I was taken by ambulance to the emergency department of the University of Flatland Hospital. I had a knee x-ray, and the attending physician told me the x-ray showed no broken bones or major fractures. He bandaged the knee and referred me to Dr. Cutworm, an orthopedic surgeon at the hospital. I had a brief visit and consultation with Dr. Cutworm the following morning. He studied the x-ray films, examined the knee briefly and in turn referred me to the Queen Victoria Hospital for an arthrogram. Dr. Cutworm told me he wanted to see if there was any cartilage or ligament damage. I went for the arthrography procedure a week after I saw Dr. Cutworm.

The arthrography procedure was uncomfortable. I felt several jabs of the needle in my bones during the procedure. I went to Dr. Cutworm's office after the results of the arthrograms were sent to him. He told me his examination of the arthrography showed that a part of my broken kneecap was floating around in the synovial fluid. He told me the broken piece could be removed by surgery, and he made arrangements for the surgical procedure.

I was admitted to the University of Flatland Hospital for the knee surgery on January 10, 1983. The surgery was not performed until January 11, 1983. In the interim, a female nurse came to my room on the evening before surgery to ask questions about my knee and my health in general. She wanted to know more about when and how I'd injured the knee. She also asked about food, medication and things I was allergic to. Most of her other questions probed into my medical history. She took my pulse, measured my blood pressure and took about six vials of blood for presurgery tests. Another nurse came to see me the following morning at about nine-thirty.

She asked the same questions and performed tests similar to the ones the first nurse had done the previous evening. The second nurse also withdrew six vials of blood from my arm. I got curious and asked why such a large volume of blood was needed. She told me they needed the blood for more tests and also to determine my blood type. The latter vials were larger than the vials the first nurse had used the previous night. I believed her story, but I wondered about the types of tests that required such a large volume of blood.

Contrary to Dr. Cutworm's estimate of two hours for the surgery, including the time for recovery from the anesthesia, I was in the operation room for more than seven hours. I woke up to find my right leg in a cast that extended from my ankle to my thigh.

Postsurgery Medical Problems

I barely slept the night after the knee surgery. The pain was unbearable. I received four injections of Demerol to relieve the pain. I was still in pain when Dr. Cutworm came to see me the next morning. The first thing he said to me was "I have bad news for you." He then told me he'd discovered the anterior cruciate ligament (ACL) on my right knee was severed, but he had not repaired it.

He gave me a prescription to relieve the pain but refused to answer any questions regarding why he had not fixed the severed anterior cruciate ligament. He came to see me again two days later to discharge me. I asked him again about the severed ligament and why there was a cast on my leg and thigh. He simply walked away from me and told me to see him in a month to have the cast removed.

I hopped around on crutches, in excruciating pain. I managed to do little work on my research and my role as a laboratory demonstrator in the department of entomology. The pain became unbearable in the third week after Dr. Cutworm discharged me. I went to his office and insisted on having the cast removed. He agreed after a brief discussion, when he realized I was in acute pain. When the cast was removed, I was horrified by the condition of my knee.

I noticed two rows of stitches on the knee. One row was about a quarter of an inch in length, and the other was almost five inches in length. The whole knee and parts of my leg and thigh were engorged with fluid. Dr. Cutworm drained most of the fluid and gave me a prescription for antibiotics. He told me that the knee might have been infected after the surgery and that the antibiotics would take care of the inflammation. He made arrangements for me to see a physiotherapist at the University of Flatland Hospital. I waited until the inflammation and pain subsided before starting physiotherapy exercises. I had to stop the exercises after a couple weeks due to the recurrence of severe inflammation and pain in the knee. The physiotherapist advised me to consult with Dr. Cutworm on the inflammation and pain for further treatment before attempting any more physiotherapy exercises. I made two attempts to see Dr. Cutworm about the pain and inflammation. On both occasions, he threatened to have me arrested by campus security if I made attempts to consult him on the problems with my knee.

When the inflammation and pain in the knee increased, I sought help from Dr. Right. Dr. Right was another orthopedic surgeon at the University of Flatland Hospital. He drained fluid from the knee and gave me a prescription for anti-inflammatory steroids to alleviate the knee problems.

A couple months after the knee surgery, I started to have acute pain in my right eye. My family physician treated the eye with various medications. When the pain and subsequent sensitivity to light persisted, he referred me to Dr. Ulysses, an ophthalmologist at the Queen Victoria Hospital in Flatland. Dr. Ulysses treated the eye with prednisone, Betagan and other medications. He could not find the cause of the eye problem and called it different names. He finally settled on acute uveitis.

In addition to my eye problem, lymph nodes all over my body became swollen ten months after the knee surgery. The inflammation and pain in my knee also continued to bother me. I was referred to Dr. Crulstein, an internist at the University of Flatland, by my family physician for further treatment of my knee and swollen lymph nodes. Initially, Dr. Crulstein treated me with high doses of colchicine. He then sent me for several x-rays of my chest, knee and both hands. Several joints of my fingers on both hands had become swollen at the same time as my nymph nodes. To treat the swollen lymph nodes, knees and fingers, Dr. Crulstein put me on high doses of prednisone. The inflammations persisted despite the steroid treatment. Dr. Crulstein then demanded and received my permission to remove two of the swollen lymph nodes from my neck for biopsy to enable him to properly diagnose the cause of my inflammation. I waited for a month to hear from Dr. Crulstein. I made several visits to his office to inquire about the result. He told me on each visit that he had not yet heard from the laboratory personnel who fixed the slides. My family physician got involved and requested that the results and the slides of the biopsy be sent to him. Dr. Crulstein refused to respond to my family physician's request. After my family physician persisted in his request, Dr. Crulstein wrote to inform us that the inflammation was due to an autoimmune disorder. My family physician and I persisted to have Dr. Crulstein release slides of the lymph nodes biopsy. He never did. He later changed his diagnosis to sarcoidosis and told my family physician the problem with the right eye was sarcoid uveitis.

Other Postsurgery Events

Department of Entomology

The year I had my knee operated on was the darkest yet in my life. Luba and I were expecting our first child in May 1983. I had to teach a laboratory class and work on my research. I was on crutches for three months due to the inflammations in my knee. The winter months were particularly hard for me. I slipped and fell down on my crutches several times. I almost hurt the left knee on one occasion during a bad slip on black ice. I took a taxi to school on days when the snowfall was too heavy for me to use my crutches.

My research work slowed to almost a halt because I could not go to the laboratory most evenings. My eye problem and swollen fingers also hindered my progress. The racial name-calling by Drs. Hierarchus, Turbulus and Twistra intensified after the knee surgery. Statements and racially degrading comments made by Drs. Turbulus and Twistra suggested to me that they knew more than I did about what had gone on during my knee surgery. Dr. Turbulus went as far as to threaten me by saying, "We will see where you get the eyes to write your thesis."

I ignored all the threats and racially explicit epithets. I was bothered by Dr. Turbulus's threat about my eyes. I suspected the problems with my right eye had originated from whatever was done to me during my knee surgery. After careful thought, I complained about Dr. Turbulus's threat to Dr. Fairhaus, another staff member in the entomology department and a member of my doctoral thesis committee.

When my complaints were brought to his attention, Dr. Turbulus denied he had ever made a derogatory comment about me or threatened me. The interpersonal conflict between Dr. Turbulus and me escalated to the point where we hardly discussed my research together. I felt uncomfortable working with him. In a desperate attempt to hurry and get the thesis done, I asked Dr. Fairhaus if he was interested in supervising my research. He declined my request. Dr. Fairhaus explained to me that changing supervisors in the middle of the research project would put strains on the friendship between him and Dr. Turbulus. He told me to keep calm, do my work and not jeopardize being awarded the degree. He also advised me against mentioning the problem between Dr. Turbulus and me at any supervisory committee meetings.

He and other members of the committee were pleased with my progress. I received constructive criticism from all the committee members except my supervisor. Dr. Turbulus stopped making derogatory remarks to me after Dr. Fairhaus told him about my complaints. He was, however, still hostile to me. He did not invite me to any of his parties. We more or less avoided each other. We communicated only when I needed his signature on a voucher to purchase items for my research. The only time we talked about my family was when we had to select a date for my candidacy examination. He found out during our discussion of the candidacy date that Luba and I were expecting our first child in May 1983. He made no comment other than to say, "I guess May is out of the question." After a brief discussion, we settled on a date for the latter part of the year, during the winter months.

I had finished my fieldwork and some laboratory experiments by the summer of 1983. I went to the department only when it was necessary to use the semi electron microscope (SEM) or the equipment in the darkroom or workshop. I spent most of the time at home, preparing for my candidacy examination. Luba and I considered taking a break and leaving Dusty Rose for a vacation in Mountain View. We needed time away from all the negative things that were going on, especially in the entomology department. Unfortunately, our finances and my health prevented us from making any trip.

The inflammation in the interior part of my right eye made the whole eye swollen despite aggressive treatment with several intraocular steroid injections by Dr. Ulysses to reduce the intraocular pressure (IOP). My right knee was swollen often. I was confined most of the time to my couch at home. Walking aggravated the pain in my knee. The other painful experience I encountered after my knee surgery was the treatment I received from some of my colleagues.

Luba and I noticed a gradual decline in interaction with friends we used to socialize with. We were informed of parties and other social functions only after they had taken place. We observed that others avoided us whenever possible. It was sad and painful to see acquaintances and friendships that had developed over the years dwindle away.

We received countless racially explicit and threatening phone calls at home. The situation was especially hard for Luba, who was pregnant. The pregnancy affected the amount of help she gave me on my research. Her help was reduced to library and typing work. She came to the department occasionally to help with my research work. The phone calls and one particular incident made her scared of being left alone at home.

The incident occurred in February after she returned home from student teaching. She had a drink of water from the fridge. She noticed that the water tasted salty, but she paid no particular attention to the taste. Shortly thereafter, she felt nauseated and started to have severe stomach cramps. She thought she was having a miscarriage. She immediately called me in the laboratory. I almost dropped the test tube in my hand when I heard her frantic cry for help over the telephone. I rushed home as fast as my crutches could carry me. She had settled down somewhat by the time I got home. I went to the fridge to taste the water, but Luba had poured it down the sink.

We waited nervously for further developments and decided to go to the hospital if she had any more stomach cramps. Apart from a slight headache, she was fine for the rest of the night. The incident made us suspicious. We resorted to arranging the items in our home to be able to detect any intrusion when we were not home. We made a petition to the housing department to relocate to the married students' complex at Culbert Hall. Luckily, our application was granted, mostly because of Luba's pregnancy.

Life in Culbert Hall was not as we expected it to be. It was like jumping from the frying pan into the fire. The unit given to us had not been cleaned after the last tenants moved out. The housing authority told us our case was an emergency, so they'd had no time to do any repair work or cleaning. They promised to have the necessary repair work and cleaning done in a month. They never showed up, despite several reminders from Luba and me. We ended up cleaning the unit.

The day after our new, unlisted phone was connected, we started receiving threatening and racially explicit calls. I informed the phone company of our problems, and they told us to inform the police. We had our phone number changed and unlisted again upon advice from the police. The calls were more frequent and vicious after the second change. We decided to ignore the comments and had to unplug our phone at bedtime to be able to sleep.

Dr. Turbulus's comments and behaviour alerted me to the possibility that a listening device had been planted in our house. Dr. Turbulus was so bent on stopping my research that he did everything to annoy me. He boasted of knowing all about my secrets and repeated some of the private conversations Luba and I had engaged in at home. My suspicion was confirmed in a curious way.

I intentionally said bad and annoying things about him at home on a Sunday evening and threatened to blow up his office. I went to his office the following Monday morning to test his reaction to my comments from the previous evening. Indeed, I was right. He was more furious than I had ever seen him. He more or less let the cat out of the bag. He repeated, word for word, all of my comments. I asked where he'd gotten his information, and he, as usual, ordered me out of his office.

I also discovered that my personal diary was an open book in the department. Drs. Hierarchus, Turbulus and Twistra repeatedly quoted phrases and comments that could only have come from people who had read my diary. I knew then that the professors had access to my briefcase. The key to my briefcase was among the set of keys that had disappeared from my office miraculously one afternoon. I'd gone to the bathroom and discovered when I returned that my keys were gone.

I discovered later that whoever had the key to my briefcase had made xeroxed copies of my diary. I saw Dr. Hierarchus with a copy of my diary. He quickly hid the papers but not before I recognized my handwriting. I learned later that the contents of my diary were one of the items the professors used to convince the doctors to hurt me. I found it difficult to believe the contents of my diary were a threat to anybody. It was my personal property, in which I wrote down my thoughts and also kept records of my research. I also included comments about progress on my research and the nonsense going on in the department. I was forced to challenge Dr. Twistra one day to stop quoting my diary. He denied having a copy of my diary. I told him in return that he must have been a psychic to be able to quote the contents of my diary word for word. My confrontation with Dr. Twistra made the already delicate situation worse. Dr. Turbulus told me on several occasions to leave the department because he was never going to award me the degree. I had learned to disregard his threats. I prepared intensely for my candidacy examination. It was the one hurdle Dr. Turbulus hoped I would not clear. I knew he was going to pull out all his tricks to make me fail the examination. I knew he would try to disturb my concentration. I knew I had to disregard all the threatening and racially explicit phone calls. I also had to turn deaf ears to the unprovoked name-calling. Briefly, I knew I had to make as little contact as possible with Dr. Turbulus. The other important event that kept Luba and me busy was the preparation for the birth of our first child.

Dr. Philemon Topas, PhD

Joy in the Midst of Adversity

We had finished with most of the preparations for the birth of our first child by the end of March 1983. We'd purchased or been given most of the items the baby would need. There was nothing fancy in the baby's room. It was functional. Luba put a mattress on the floor for breastfeeding at night. She did not breastfeed in our bedroom in order not to disturb my sleep. My candidacy examination was tentatively scheduled for September or October. Members of the supervisory committee made the decision on the exact date for the examination. I needed all the sleep I could get. I had to be well rested to concentrate during my preparation for the examination.

I maintained a calm and positive attitude in anticipation of our baby's birth and my examination. I could not spend as much time as I would have liked on my studies because I had to help Luba around the house. She had grown a large stomach and found it tiring and difficult to move around the house. The latter half of March and the whole month of April were particularly difficult times for her. She rested most of the time, and I was by her side most of the time. It was interesting and refreshing to feel and see the baby move around in her womb. We were both excited about the baby. We played fun games in selecting a name, and we were thrilled about becoming parents.

We enjoyed going to birthing classes together at the University of Flatland Hospital. Sharing the company of other parents and would-be parents was helpful. We learned important and useful lessons from couples who'd had children. The group sessions alleviated most of our worries and made Luba feel more at ease about delivering the baby. I also learned a lot and had a good idea of what to expect. The film sessions were most informative. I knew our car had to be in good mechanical shape. It was necessary to have the items she would need in the hospital packed and ready to go. I was glad I attended the classes and other sessions. As a result, I was less anxious, slept better and was better prepared for the delivery. We waited expectantly. We knew the end of April was countdown time. I prayed she would have a safe delivery and gave Luba nightly massages. May finally arrived, and despite all our preparations, my level of anxiety increased. I could hardly sleep. I could tell from Luba's behaviour that the delivery day was around the corner. I had purchased a special card for Luba in anticipation of Mother's Day. I was eager to give her the card at the restaurant where I had arranged for a special dinner for two.

On May 6, a couple days before Mother's Day, the baby rotated to the birthing position. We knew then that it was a matter of days until the delivery. We spent most of the next day at Boat Ride Park. Luba wanted to watch birds and ducks fly around. We fed them bread, as we always did whenever we visited the park. Her behaviour was unusual. I suspected the baby was sending the signal of "Here I come." We spent most of the following day at Boat Ride Park again. It was a beautiful park. It had a central lake that was a favourite skating rendezvous for lovers and families in the winter. In the summer months, the lake was used mostly by teenagers for sports fishing. Our favourite activity on the lake was going for boat rides. We did not go for a paddleboat ride that day. Luba was not in the mood. She spent most of the time sleeping and feeding birds and ducks. We took pictures of the birds in their moment of hunger. They crowded around us in their attempts to eat the bread pieces we fed them. We returned home just in time for supper. Luba barely ate that evening, and her behaviour was unusual. She told me the baby was moving around a lot. I kept a close watch over her. She woke me up at four o'clock in the morning when her water broke. We were at the University of Flatland Hospital by four-thirty.

Naomi, a healthy baby girl weighing 7 pounds and 14 ounces, was delivered around ten-thirty that evening. She was beautiful and even gave me a smile. Luba could not have wished for a better Mother's Day present. The birth of Naomi made me more relaxed. I was able to pay more attention to my preparation for the candidacy examination. I made an adjustment to my schedule. I got up early, usually at four-thirty, and did most of my studies. I also spent more time in the library. My new schedule was helpful.

Naomi was a welcome addition to our family. Luba and I were glad to have her, and we spent most evenings playing with her. She cried a lot and did not like to sleep on her own. She was more at ease when held in our arms. Her constant crying and sleeplessness left us exhausted. Her ear infections were frequent and persisted, at times, for more than a month. Her sleeping pattern settled down after about 11 months. I was close to her and was delighted to see her grow. She used to wait by the living room window for me when I returned home from the library. She somehow knew I usually came home at six-thirty for dinner, and she was excited when she saw me coming. Her high chair was close to me at the dining table. I gave her bits and pieces of my dinner against Luba's objection. The three of us became buddies. We had to rearrange our living room when she started to crawl. She was into everything within her reach. She loved to open the doors of the kitchen cupboards and play with cooking pots. Her presence had a positive effect on my studies. I knew she enjoyed playing with me at home, so I made good use of my time in the library.

PhD Candidacy Examination and Language Proficiency Test

After Naomi was born, Dr. Turbulus and I got together and chose the third week of October 1983 as the date for my candidacy examination. He congratulated me on the occasion of Naomi's birth and gave Luba and me a beautiful, soft sheepskin for the baby's crib. Dr. Turbulus's attitude toward me changed temporarily for the better soon after Naomi was born. He and I were able to relate both socially and academically. We re-established our mentor-student relationship, and I was glad about the turn of events. Unfortunately, the good time was short-lived. For reasons I hitherto do not understand, Dr. Turbulus's attitude changed toward me again just around the time of my candidacy examination. The sudden change in his attitude troubled me, but I resolved not to let it disturb my preparation for the examination.

The day of the examination was a good one for me. We had a mild, above-average temperature for an October day in western Multizone. I knew when I woke up that I was going to have a good day. The examination was scheduled for 3:00 p.m. I spent a good part of the morning at home, playing with my daughter. Naomi woke us up most mornings at about seven o'clock, mostly because she wanted to eat and play with us. She repeated her waking-up routine on the day of my examination with her usual "Dada, Mama-ooh" song. I left home after lunch and spent some time in the library to look over my notes one more time before the examination.

Things went well during the examination. The committee members were familiar to me, and their jovial attitude helped me get rid of my nervousness. After the formalities, which included the format and order of questioning, we got down to serious business. Most of the questions were on aquatic invertebrate ecology and were framed within the context of evolutionary biology. There were also questions on experimental design and the relationship among structural design of organisms, function and behaviour. The questioning ended at about five o'clock.

I was asked to leave the examination room while the committee members deliberated on my performance. They called me back after about 20 minutes and told me the committee had unanimously agreed that I passed the examination. They pointed out a few glitches in some of my responses, and then they all congratulated me. I thanked them, quietly let out a sigh of relief and rushed home to give Luba and Naomi the good news. Luba prepared a special meal that evening to celebrate the occasion. Naomi did not understand why Luba and I were in such a happy and joyous mood. She laughed with us, and sensing I was in a happy mood, she demanded I play her favourite game, hide-and-seek, with her.

Luba and I stayed up late that night. She wanted to know what had gone on during the examination. She was particularly curious about Dr. Turbulus's behaviour. We also talked about my foreign language examination, which was the next hurdle. One of the requirements of the PhD program was the demonstration of proficiency in a foreign language. I'd chosen French for a couple reasons. I had studied the language in high school and knew I would not have to put in too much time and effort to pass the examination. The other reason was that several publications in the French language were relevant to my research. I wanted to be able to translate those papers into English. The language proficiency examination was scheduled for the week before the Christmas break.

I learned from the French professor who was going to administer the examination that I would be required to translate a French publication relevant to my area of research into English. I had spent some of the time during my preparation for the candidacy examination polishing up my French. I knew I would not have to put in as much time and effort as I had for the candidacy examination in order to pass the French examination. Based on those two factors, I decided to take a week off from studying and spend the time with Luba and Naomi. The three of us spent most of the week at Boat Ride Park and in one of the malls in Dusty Rose.

The mall was spectacular and huge. It was the biggest mall in the world until 1989, when the owners, a group of Middle Eastern oil magnates, built a bigger mall in Grandonia. The Dusty Rose mall successfully combined commerce with pleasure. In addition to a spacious indoor wave pool, which had a large, sandy beach with palm trees, several other entertainment venues were in the mall. Naomi's favourite place in the mall was the section with all sorts of rides, especially the merry-go-round. She also enjoyed looking at the exotic birds in a glass cage. I was refreshed after the week I spent with my family. I intensified my preparation for the foreign language examination after the brief break. The French translation took place at the scheduled time. I had no problem with the examination.

Application for Multizonian Immigration Papers

With the candidacy examination and foreign language requirement behind me and with most of my research work completed, I decided to pay more attention to my application to stay in Multizone. I had applied for Multizonian immigration papers in March 1983, three months after Luba and I were married. I had known when I submitted my application that I had to return to Nugget River to honour the five-year bond I had entered into with the government of Nugget River when I was awarded the scholarship in 1977. I was supposed to return to Nugget River after completing my PhD studies to be employed with the Kilan River Basin Research Authority in Cascade Falls as a research scientist. The organization had sponsored my application for the scholarship. I also knew Luba and I wanted to return to Multizone after I completed my obligation to the government of Nugget River. We planned on raising our family in Multizone, and I planned to become a citizen of Multizone eventually. Having Multizonian immigration papers did not violate the terms of my bond. The immigration papers were to facilitate our plans to return to Multizone after we served the Nugget River government.

Immigration authorities in Dusty Rose, Flatland, informed me in September 1983, six long months after I'd submitted my application, that my application would be processed within Multizone on humanitarian grounds. We were given an appointment for an interview with immigration authorities in May 1984. I called the immigration office several times in January and February 1984 to find out the nature of the impending interview.

We had the interview a few days after the three of us celebrated Naomi's first birthday. Naomi was with us at the interview. She was still being breastfed. The interview took about an hour. After the interview, the immigration authorities informed me that I had to undergo a new medical examination because my application could not be processed with the records of the 1977 medical examination used to admit me to Multizone. I tried unsuccessfully to find out why my old medical records could not be used, since I had remained in Multizone all the time up to my interview. I had not travelled to any country with endemic disease that would threaten Multizonian citizens. I found out later that my 1977 medical records should have been used for my landed immigrant application.

Nevertheless, I was given a list of medical doctors who performed medical examinations for the immigration department and told to have one of them examine me and send them the results of my examination. I went for the medical examination shortly after the interview, and the results were submitted to the immigration authorities in the last week of May 1984.

While waiting to hear from the immigration authorities, I managed to round up all my research work and start writing my dissertation. I stayed away from the entomology department as much as I could. Dr. Turbulus and some other members of faculty learned of my application for Multizonian immigration papers from a source I hitherto have not found out. The information fuelled the level of Dr. Turbulus's animosity and hostile behaviour toward me. I had in an inexplicable way become immune to the unprovoked, brutal and hurtful behaviour. My objective, especially after passing both the candidacy and foreign language examinations, was within reach, and I made every effort to stay focused. I knew I had but one more hurdle to clear: the thesis defense. Naomi's presence also helped me to stay focused on earning the degree. The knowledge that she, and the other children we planned on having, would have to be fed and educated was the impetus I needed to go on.

I avoided all contact with the entomology department and chose instead to write my thesis in the computer lab at the students' residence where we lived. I saw Dr. Turbulus only when it was absolutely necessary. Meeting with him became difficult and uncomfortable for me. I had to psych myself up and be ready for rude and racially degrading comments. I was scared because I had never met anybody who hated me as much as he did. I knew of hate groups that killed and lynched people. My fear intensified when I was alone with him. I was afraid he might attack me and defend himself by saying I'd first attacked him. After all, our problems were openly known and talked about in the entomology department. I saw him only when I needed more money in my computer account or needed to discuss the possible times the thesis would be ready to be defended. He informed me during one of our rare meetings that he had talked to Dr. Flowtus, a foremost authority on biological fluid mechanics. He was a professor at Prize University in Grandonia. I had read most of his numerous publications. His latest book was a gem and a masterpiece on biofluid mechanics. The book had been published in time for me to benefit greatly from its contents and references. Dr. Turbulus informed me of the possible dates Dr. Flowtus could come as the external examiner for the defense of my thesis. The thesis had to be sent to him at least a month before the defense date.

I knew I could have a preliminary draft of the thesis ready by the end of August or early September 1984. My write-up was moving along quickly, partly because I had written up a large portion of the thesis in the fall of 1982. As I mentioned before, Dr. Turbulus had ordered me to do so due to the false reports he'd received from the agricultural research station in Hill Point. I'd been bitter and unhappy about doing it in 1982, but I was glad I had. I was able to get the preliminary draft copy to Dr. Turbulus and the other members of my supervisory committee at the end of August 1984. The comments and corrections of the committee were helpful and enabled me to improve the quality of subsequent drafts. I was excited when Dr. Turbulus informed me that Dr. Flowtus was coming at the end of November 1984. The thesis was at a stage where the supervisory committee and I felt I needed Dr. Flowtus's comments and corrections before I could prepare a final draft.

I would have met Dr. Flowtus and some other biomechanics researchers during summer school at the experimental station in Scottsdale Harbor. One of the experts, Dr. Garvinchi, a professor in the department of evolutionary biology at the University of Rich Town, had invited me to attend the summer school in 1983. Financial and time constraints had prevented me from attending. I'd wanted to be home to help Luba and spend time with Naomi. I also had been preparing for my candidacy examination and could not afford to take any time off. I was fortunate to meet Dr. Garvinchi when he came to the zoology department at the University of Flatland to deliver a series of seminars on biomechanics.

Defense of PhD Dissertation

While waiting for Dr. Flowtus for the defense of my dissertation, I made several calls and visits to the Multizonian immigration office in Dusty Rose to inquire about the status of my application. They'd told me in May 1984, when I'd submitted the results of the medical examination, they would notify me of the outcome of my application at the end of August 1984. The Dusty Rose office kept telling me the immigration department in Looney Bay had not yet made a decision on my application. I requested to have a meeting with the manager of the Dusty Rose office, but the office turned down my request. I was able to speak to her on the phone, however. She told me the delay in reviewing my application was because Looney Bay had a backlog of cases to work on. She promised to instruct the officer handling my file to send the Looney Bay office a reminder to speed up the processing of my application. I did not make any other attempts to inquire about my application after my telephone conversation with the manager of the Dusty Rose office. I realized I was not making any headway with the immigration authorities, and the time I spent calling and visiting their office was a distraction to my preparations for the defense of my thesis.

I focused on reviewing my thesis and researching sections of the research that would require further explaining and thus generate debate. I was confident about my methodology. My data and the manner in which I interpreted them was consistent with current thought in the field. Areas of the work I expected to defend were those that dealt with the use of scaled-up physical models. I also expected to spend some time talking about the contribution of the work to the field of biofluid mechanics and the future research my results would generate. Of course, I also expected my knowledge of past and current literature and research in my area of specialization to be tested.

Dr. Flowtus arrived the day prior to my defense. He was a few hours late due to a snowstorm that delayed his flight at the airport in Grandonia. He spent the night at Dr. Turbulus's house. I socialized briefly with him and other members of my supervisory committee at Dr. Turbulus's house in the evening. He gave a seminar in the entomology department just before lunch. I was impressed by his presentation and the contents of his seminar. I had enjoyed and benefited greatly from reading his publications. Hearing him speak gave me a greater appreciation for his talent and genius. I was one of those who asked him a question when Dr. Turbulus, who chaired the seminar, opened the seminar to questions. After Dr. Flowtus responded to my question, Dr. Turbulus quipped, "Oh, Philemon, I guess you've fired the first shot at your external examiner." The audience and I burst out in laughter. Dr. Flowtus jokingly responded, "Philemon just got me to answer one of the questions I was going to ask him this afternoon." Again, there was laughter in the audience. Dr. Turbulus's and Dr. Flowtus's comments calmed my nerves and took care of my jitters. I had lunch with Dr. Flowtus and members of the committee, and we shared a few more jokes over lunch.

The examination was scheduled for 3:00 p.m., and we started on time. Everything went well during my thesis defense. I was questioned on areas I'd expected. I also faced some questions I had not thought about, but I handled them well. Dr. Flowtus was friendly during the examination. His comments on the research were mostly positive, although he had a surprisingly long list of suggestions and corrections, which kept me busy for weeks after the defense. I thought I had caught most of the errors in the write-up. His suggestions for improving the thesis were helpful. He was not happy about the way I'd done a few things, but his overall comment was that the research was impressive. He recommended the work be accepted after I made all corrections.

Dr. Turbulus and the other members of the committee also made suggestions that helped improve the thesis. We were done just before six o'clock. I went home and gave Luba and Naomi the good news. I prepared a quick dinner for Naomi and myself because I had to be at Dr. Turbulus's house at seven-thirty for a mixer to celebrate my successful defense and to thank Dr. Flowtus and the members of the supervisory committee for their help. I wished I could have gone to the mixer with Luba, but she had grown another tummy. She was in the last trimester of her pregnancy with our second child, and she was not feeling well that evening.

Most of my colleagues, all the members of my supervisory committee and most of the faculty in the entomology department were at the mixer. Other students and faculty from the zoology department also came to the mixer as the evening progressed. Dr. Flowtus was kept busy most of the evening. I managed to talk with him just before he withdrew to bed. His flight back to Grandonia the next day was leaving early in the morning, and he wanted to get some sleep before leaving.

He suggested I write to Dr. Garvinchi at the University of Rich Town to inquire about the possibility of postdoctoral studies in his laboratory. He also promised to recommend me to Dr. Garvinchi. I told him I would keep in touch with him and send him any publications that came out of the thesis. He thanked me for promising to send the publications and told me, "Keep working hard, and I hope you will continue to do more work with moving fluids." The mixer ended at about two o'clock in the morning, a few hours after Dr. Flowtus went to bed.

Having cleared the final hurdle, I knew my objective was within reach. I wasted no time in going to work on making the corrections and incorporating the ideas suggested by Dr. Flowtus and the members of my supervisory committee. My deteriorating health, especially the progressive loss of sight in my right eye, was another reason I wanted to hurry to submit the thesis. I needed medical attention, and I was worried I might not be able to submit the thesis on time if I was admitted to hospital.

Time was of the essence for a number of important reasons. I wanted to graduate in June 1985. I had to submit three copies of my thesis to the office of graduate studies by March 31, 1985, to be included in the June convocation assembly. Dr. Turbulus had mentioned to me on several occasions that he was running out of funds and wanted me to be done by the end of March 1985. He did stop supporting me at the end of March. I was fortunate to get funds for three months from the dean of graduate studies and from a part-time laboratory demonstrator position in the department of genetics. I managed to save enough money to support my family. The most important reason time was a limiting factor was the due date of our second child.

The Birth of Our Second Child

Luba was expected to deliver in mid-January 1985, and I wanted to have more time to spend with Luba and the two children. Zevin was delivered on February 1, 1985. He arrived two weeks after his due date. He was quite a load at 9 pounds and 14 ounces. His arrival did not cause any delay in my meeting the March 31 deadline for getting two bound copies and one unbound copy of my completed thesis to the office of graduate studies. To meet the deadline, I spent daylight hours with my family and worked on my thesis during most of the nocturnal hours after the kids went to bed. I submitted my thesis a week ahead of the deadline date. My next task was to pack the rest of my equipment and books and move permanently out of the entomology department at the end of March 1985. With my dissertation out of the way, I had much time to devote to my family. I also prepared and made arrangements for my convocation ceremony.

Naomi and Zevin brought much joy to Luba and me. The four of us were together most of the times, and we savoured every second of it. We spent a lot of time at home because of the cold weather and waited impatiently for summer. Luba and I observed a change in Naomi's behaviour after we brought Zevin home. She became quieter and less playful. At first, we were worried and thought she was not feeling well. After carefully watching her, we noticed that her sudden change in behaviour occurred whenever Luba and I shared her toys and our time with Zevin. She was not happy about the time and attention we gave to Zevin. But who could blame her? She was used to getting our full and unshared attention and found it difficult to adjust to the presence of another baby in the house. Luba and I were relieved when we discovered the cause of her behaviour. We understood her and made some changes in the way we interacted with both of them, being careful not to show any favouritism. We were patient with her, and our patience produced a positive result with time. She started playing with her brother, and it was fun to see the two of them interact. They shared toys, messed up the house and had disagreements. Zevin, as expected, ended up with the shorter end of the stick when a disagreement became physical. The times I spent with my family also helped to relieve my worry and anxiety over my deteriorating health and my problems with the immigration authorities. The latter problem was more of an irritation than something that made me anxious.

Convocation Ceremony

My convocation ceremony was colourful. We had nice, pleasant June weather on the day of the ceremony. I was one of the 400 students at the convocation ceremony. The convocation hall, which could seat 1,200, was filled to capacity. Invited guests, proud parents who'd come to see their children graduate and other personnel associated with the ceremony accounted for the rest of the audience. Luba was there with our two children and her mom and dad. I was excited to see the sea of people gathered for the occasion. My PhD convocation was my first one. I had not attended my BS convocation ceremony at the University of Nugget River. I had travelled to Aurus immediately after the results of my final examination were published. I'd been unable to wait to share the good news about my success with my family in Aurus. We had been away from each other for a long time. I'd wanted them to know their investment in my education had produced good results. My MS convocation at Amicus University had taken place when I was at the

University of Flatland in Dusty Rose. I'd left Amicus University soon after I finished my fieldwork. I'd submitted my MS thesis three months after my convocation.

Watching all the jubilation and pomp going on around me during the convocation ceremony at the University of Flatland made me regret not being present at my previous two convocations. I knew then that I had missed occasions dedicated to the celebration of success and sharing in the joy that crowned hard work. I knew also that I could not make up for the two lost opportunities, so I made sure to savour every moment of the ceremony. My family and Luba's parents went to our apartment after the convocation to continue the celebration. We had coffee and socialized until after dinner, when Luba's parents left. They congratulated me and gave me $500. I was glad to see Luba's parents at my convocation.

The convocation made me more aware that success was an important value all human beings longed for. The smiles, hugs, congratulatory speeches and picture taking in the recognition of an achievement gave me hope and reassured my belief in the human spirit. I saw a human quality that told me there was hope for the survival of the human race despite the dehumanization and bashing I'd undergone in the entomology department at the University of Flatland. I knew I would never forget my ordeal in the entomology department. The things I saw at the convocation ceremony made me swear never to stoop to the level of savagery to which some humans, such as those I'd encountered in the entomology department, had degenerated. My observations at the convocation made me more determined to exert more pressure on the immigration authorities. I saw a similarity between the way they were treating me and what had happened at the University of Flatland. I had had enough of people who lacked respect for their fellow humans and who would do things to hurt or impede their human need for success.

CHAPTER 6
Postgraduation Events

Problems with Application for Multizonian Immigration Papers

I still had not heard from the immigration department at the end of March 1985. I visited their office several times only to be given the same answer: "We have not yet heard from Looney Bay about your application. We will call you as soon as we hear from them." I suspected that something might have gone wrong with the application. After a few more visits to the Dusty Rose office, I asked to be given the name and phone number of the officer in the immigration department in Looney Bay who was handling my file. My attempts to find out the cause of the delay from the Looney Bay office produced no results. The delay in hearing from the Multizonian immigration authorities became a problem for Luba and me. We knew our plans to return to Multizone after my service in Nugget River would be affected if I did not receive my Multizonian immigration papers before leaving for Nugget River. We were also concerned about my health. We talked about how safe it would be for me to go into an environment with numerous endemic diseases. I needed treatment, and the doctors had not found the cause of my ill health; thus, Luba and I were concerned about going to Nugget River. We knew the treatment I required, if any was available, would more likely be found in Multizone and be better than in Nugget River. After serious deliberation, we decided I should try to get the Multizonian immigration papers before going to Nugget

River. We were worried about my health and wanted to be sure I would be able to return immediately to Multizone or Grandonia if my health deteriorated while I was in Nugget River. Luba and I knew we had until June to put more pressure on the immigration authorities to give me an answer about my application. We called their office often. In mid-April 1985, 11 months after submitting my application, I received a call from the Dusty Rose office.

I recognized the voice on the other end of the line as that of the immigration officer I had spoken with on countless occasions. He congratulated me and added, "We finally heard from Looney Bay about your application yesterday evening. Your application has not been rejected. We do, however, have problems with your medical examination. You did not pass the medical examination because you have sarcoidosis, and in accordance with immigration rules, you are not admissible to Multizone at this time. You have a medical condition that would make you a burden on the health and welfare system." Upon my further inquiry, he told me I would receive an official letter detailing the decision of the immigration department concerning my application. Luba and I were terribly disappointed about the news. We decided to withhold our comments and reactions until after we received the immigration minister's letter.

We waited anxiously for a week until the letter was delivered. The contents of the letter confirmed our suspicion that the immigration department's delay in notifying us of their decision on my application had been planned. The timing of the notification, we felt, was to frustrate us and make it difficult for me to return to Multizone. In his letter, the minister mentioned that a section of the immigration law required that people in my situation be given a special permit. The permit would be renewed annually for five years. In the interim, the minister would consider granting me Multizonian immigration papers if my health improved enough to enable me to pass the immigration medical examination. If I was not able to pass the required medical examination within the five-year period, then my case would be considered at that time, and an appropriate decision would be made.

We contacted the Dusty Rose office to ask for clarification on what "being a burden on the health and welfare system" meant. In response to our inquiry, we were told that immigration doctors expected my condition to further deteriorate and prevent me from making a living. The doctors were also concerned the cost of taking care of me would be too high for the health system to afford. I informed my family doctor about the comments of the immigration authorities. He was surprised to hear about the conclusion reached by the doctors who'd performed my immigration health examination. He assured me my health would not deteriorate to the extent of incapacitating me. He also disagreed with the statement on the cost of providing medical care for me. He said, "There are a lot of people in this country whose medical treatment and maintenance far exceed the cost of treating sarcoidosis, if that is what you are suffering from. You do not and will not require treatment beyond that which is given to most Multizonians." He was concerned there might be other reasons I was being denied Multizonian immigration papers.

We had a discussion about what he could do to help me in addition to the treatment I was receiving from him and from an ophthalmologist, Dr. Ulysses, to whom he had referred me in 1983. We agreed I should be referred to Dr. Goldberg, an internist who was a specialist in sarcoidosis. While waiting to see Dr. Goldberg in July, I went to the immigration office for the special permit at the end of May 1985.

My impatience with the immigration department made the time I spent waiting to see Dr. Goldberg unpleasant. In the interim, my impatience and frustration affected my relationship with Luba and our two children. Our times together ceased to be joyful to me. All I wanted to do was see my family doctor and Dr. Goldberg and resolve my problems with the immigration authorities. A few days before my appointment with Dr. Goldberg, my family doctor requested a letter from Dr. Ulysses, the ophthalmologist who was treating my eye problem. The letter was to inform Dr. Goldberg of the treatment I was receiving from Dr. Ulysses.

My first visit with Dr. Goldberg was brief. He asked me a few questions, took samples of my blood and urine and had me go for x-rays of my chest. He informed me he had received reports of the treatment I'd received from my family doctor and Drs. Ulysses and Crulstein. At our next meeting a week later, Dr. Goldberg informed me he had carefully studied the reports from the other doctors. Along with the urine and blood tests and a chest x-ray, he sent me for a lung function test. The test was done a few hours later in the same building where he had his office. He studied the results of the lung function test and told me I should stop taking high oral doses of prednisolone, which had been prescribed by Dr. Crulstein. According to Dr. Goldberg, my chest x-ray and lung function indicated that my sarcoidosis, or whatever reason Dr. Crulstein had had for prescribing such high doses of prednisolone, was under good control or was in remission. However, he agreed with Dr. Ulysses, the ophthalmologist, that I had to continue to use 1 percent prednisolone and Betagan for the pain and inflammation in my right eye. In his opinion, the occasional intraocular cortisone injections should be continued to reduce inflammation in the posterior part of my eye. He made a request for slides of my lymph node biopsies from Dr. Crulstein, but the slides were not sent to him.

Relocation to Looney Bay, December 1985

The headquarters of the Multizonian immigration centre were located in Looney Bay, and that played a major role in our decision to relocate there. We wanted to go petition the minister of immigration personally. We sold most of our possessions when the welfare department refused to help us relocate to Looney Bay because my wife's parents were in Dusty Rose. Welfare department policy was to keep welfare recipients close to their immediate families. My wife's parents had given us as much help as they could afford. We decided not to ask them for more help. We reasoned that if the minister of immigration turned down our petition, then we would try to relocate to Grandonia, Derkland or Crimson after my service to the Nugget River government. A more urgent reason for our deciding to leave Dusty Rose was the increase in the frequency of threatening phone calls and acts of violence we experienced. The straw that broke the camel's back, so to say, was the night empty wine and beer bottles were smashed on our front doorstep and lawn. We wanted to leave the week after the bottle-smashing incident, but the inexplicable disappearance of my passport delayed our departure.

I kept the passport in the inside pocket of my suit jacket in our bedroom closet. The last time I'd seen the passport had been a few days before my convocation. I only put on formal attire on rare and special occasions. My convocation had been one of those occasions, and I'd decided to wear my one and only suit. The passport had still been in the inside pocket when I put the suit back in the closet after the convocation ceremony. The bottle-smashing incident occurred one week after my convocation.

I discovered that the passport was not in the pocket of the suit jacket when my family was getting ready for a convocation party to which a friend had invited us. Luba and I turned our apartment upside down in search of the passport. We did not find it. We reported the disappearance of the passport to the police, and an officer came over to investigate the case. He told us it was strange that no other items were missing from the apartment. He gave us his card and told us to let him know if we found the passport.

I informed the Nugget River High Commission in Looney Bay of the disappearance of my passport and asked for a replacement. The high commission sympathized with me and told me I needed to have the police send them their report before they could send me application forms for a new passport. They also wanted me to pay a passport fee of $250 Grandonian, but they waived the fee after I informed them I was sponsored by the government of Nugget River to study in Multizone. The police refused to send the report to the Nugget River High Commission. I was informed that it was the police department's policy not to send reports of their investigations to foreign governments.

The bottle-smashing incident happened during the time I was trying to find ways to have the police report sent to the Nugget River High Commission or given to me. We feared greatly for our safety and became prisoners in our own home. After we found out the passport was gone, we noticed someone had forced entry into our apartment through a kitchen window. Luba and I noticed the forced entry after careful inspection of the door lock and the window locks. We discovered that the netting of one kitchen window had been ripped off and hastily tucked back into the seal. The netting came loose with the slightest tug on it, unlike the other window settings. We were scared to leave our apartment unattended. The incident rekindled the fear and terror we'd dealt with after we discovered our house had been broken into when we were students. The police gave me the report after several appeals at the end of July 1985. We left Dusty Rose at the end of August 1985.

The trip to Looney Bay took eight days and was plagued with problems. We left Dusty Rose at dawn in a car Luba's parents had sold to us for one dollar. The car was a gift, but the law required we pay at least a dollar to be able to register it in our name and purchase insurance. Luba; her twin sister, Lena; and their older sister used to drive the car before we took possession of it. Luba's dad and I spent three days in his garage, building a sturdy and large carrier on the roof of the car for our luggage. Our itinerary included a stopover at Bunnyfields to spend the night with Luba's grandparents and aunts and uncles. We had car problems when we were about 80 kilometres from the farm where Luba's relatives lived.

We called the farm, and one of Luba's aunts came to pick us up. The car was towed to a garage, and we learned the following morning that the engine had overheated and was seriously damaged. The mechanic thought he might be able to fix the engine if he could get replacements for the damaged parts. He told us it would take him a couple days to determine the extent of the damage before he could tell us how much it would cost to fix the engine. I called Dr. Godfather, whom we had arranged to stay with in Looney Bay until we found an apartment. While waiting to hear from the mechanic, I informed Dr. Godfather of our car problems and promised to let him know when we would be in Looney Bay. We also spent the time making the acquaintance of Luba's relatives. Her grandpa became fond of me, and we spent most of the time together. It was the first time we had met since Luba and I got married. We had a lot of catching up to do on what had transpired since our marriage. He told me stories about the farm, which his dad had handed down to him. He was satisfied with the way he and his sons managed the farm and wished the farm would always remain in his family. He played with Naomi and Zevin most evenings. He was particularly fond of Zevin and told us Zevin looked like the type he would love to have on the farm because of his bulk and musculature. Indeed, even for an 8-month-old boy, Zevin had good muscle tone—I guess mostly because of good care and his constant crawling and moving around. Luba spent most of her time with her grandma. It was just about the harvest season, and Luba's uncles were busy getting the combine and other things ready. We could not spend as much time as we would have liked with them. We met with them and their families some evenings. Our family and the others had fun sharing dinner and conversation.

The news from the mechanic was not encouraging. He'd discovered after taking a closer look that the damage was more extensive than he had anticipated. It was still fixable, but he would have to order parts from the capital city of Bunnyfields. The parts would take a day to arrive, and the cost of the repair would be about $2,500 Multizonian. Luba and I did not have that amount of money, and we did not want to burden her relatives with the cost of fixing our car. After thinking about the cost of the repair and the extra time it would take, we decided against fixing the car. We told Luba's relatives to have the car towed to the farm, fix it if they wanted to and then keep it.

We considered alternative means of getting to Looney Bay. Fortunately for us, one of Luba's uncles was a part-time worker with Multizonian National Railway. He made arrangements for us to continue our trip to Looney Bay. I called Dr. Godfather and told him to expect us in a couple days. We boarded the train at twelve-thirty in the morning on the sixth day after our arrival on the farm. The four of us were able to catch up on sleep when some rows of seats were vacated by passengers at their destinations. We were fortunate to have those seats for most of the trip to Looney Bay.

We arrived in Looney Bay on September 2, 1985. I called Dr. Godfather when we arrived. He came with his wife, Elizabeth, to pick us up within half an hour of my call. Dr. Godfather, you will recall, was the entomologist who'd helped me with my MS research on apple orchard insects. I had maintained correspondence with him after I graduated from the Sunnydale campus of Amicus University. Dr. Godfather, Dr. Howard and I had coauthored a publication from my MS dissertation in 1982.

Dr. Godfather and Elizabeth were nice to my family. He was still working at the arthropod history and identification research station in Looney Bay. He was at work most of the time. After recuperating from the trip and settling in at Dr. Godfather's house, Luba and I embarked on searching for an apartment on the third day after we arrived. Our first order of business was to go to the social services department to apply for social assistance. We then bought a map of the city and the local newspaper. After a whole day's search, mostly by telephone calls, we found no apartment. The apartments listed for rent were either too expensive for our meagre welfare budget or not for rent to families with children. Having failed to get anything through the newspaper, we resorted to networking with housing management companies. The problems we encountered with the companies were bizarre.

Some companies sent us on wild goose chases to addresses that did not exist. The apartment managers to whom we were referred were the most frustrating part of dealing with management companies. Most of the managers either would not return our calls or were never home when we made arrangements to come see the vacant units. We became frustrated after more than a week of fruitless, tiring efforts to get an apartment. Dr. Godfather and Elizabeth got involved in helping us, but even our combined efforts produced no results. It became unspeakably embarrassing when we found ourselves still at Dr. Godfather's house two weeks later. Luba and I had expected to be in our own apartment a week after we arrived in Looney Bay.

Dr. Godfather and Elizabeth did not express discomfort at our presence in their home, but Luba and I knew the house was overcrowded with seven people. Ken, Dr. Godfather's younger son, was away most of the day at medical school, but we felt that two weeks was enough, and we had to move somewhere else. Dr. Godfather and Elizabeth were not happy when we informed them of our decision to move to the nearby YMCA and YWCA building. We insisted on moving and thanked them for their hospitality. Our accommodations at the YMCA and YWCA building were livable and enabled Luba and me to pursue our two main objectives for coming to Looney Bay.

We went to the immigration office and hand-delivered a letter in which we requested a meeting with a senior immigration officer. While waiting to hear from the department of immigration, I made an appointment to see the head of chancery at the Nugget River High Commission in September. The purpose of my appointment was to deliver the police report on my missing passport. I also wanted to have arrangements made for my family and me to return to Nugget River to honour the five-year bond I had entered into with the government. I did not know what response to expect concerning the second objective of my appointment. The government of Nugget River had changed the terms of the bond and reneged on supporting me until I completed my studies.

The Nugget River High Commission told me in August 1984 to wind up my PhD studies at the end of that year and return to Nugget River. They informed me there was an urgent need for lecturers in the universities, and my failure to meet the deadline would result in the termination of my award. They made the decision to change the terms of the bond without prior notice to me or to the Kilan River Basin Research Authority in Cascade Falls, who originally had sponsored my application for the scholarship. As I said, I was supposed to return to Cascade Falls to work as a research scientist after my studies. I was also in the midst of preparing my dissertation when I received the high commission's letter. I informed them of the terms of my bond and the status of my dissertation and asked to be given between six to eight months to complete and defend the thesis. They turned down my request. I was lucky I had extra finances from my graduate teaching assistantship in the entomology department. Luba also chipped in some of her student loan money to enable us to support our family and to allow me to complete and defend my thesis in June 1985.

In mid-September, I received the immigration department's response concerning my request to see one of their senior officers, and it was encouraging. They wanted me to go for another medical examination before they would review my file. The time constraints coupled with the fact that I submitted the result of the new medical examination to the immigration office in Dusty Rose shortly before our departure made me refuse to go for the examination. I decided to stop pursuing the immigration application and concentrate my efforts on going back to Nugget River.

I was on time for my appointment with the head of chancery at the Nugget River High Commission. I knew the high commission had relocated to another address during my correspondence with them. The new location was a house and was more spacious than the old address I'd visited when I was at Amicus University. I was impressed by the setup.

The secretary and guest waiting rooms were on the ground floor. The high commissioner and other senior staff occupied the upstairs section of the building. After a brief introduction, the secretary informed the head of chancery of my arrival. I waited for a few minutes and was directed to his office. I found out he had been at the high commission since 1983. His predecessor had been either called back to Nugget River or assigned to another high commission. I am not sure on the details of what he told me about his predecessor. We touched on different interesting topics, some of which dealt with how Nugget River had changed since I left in 1977. I waited until after we finished coffee before I told him of my desire to return to Nugget River.

He wanted to know if I had been awarded the PhD degree. I gave him details of the colourful convocation ceremony and shared my regret of missing my previous two convocations with him. I then informed him I was married and had two children. He was glad to hear about my family and wanted to know if they were in Looney Bay with me. After giving an affirmative response, I told him my wife and the children would love to see Gondwana and be glad to spend time with my family. I then asked him how long it would take for arrangements to be made for my family and me to go back to Cascade Falls. At that point in our conversation, he told me he wanted to take a quick look at my file. After looking through my file, he asked me to wait in his office while he had a brief consultation with the ambassador. He came back after about 20 minutes to inform me that the high commission did not have the funds to send my family and me back to Nugget River. I wanted to know if the scholarship secretariat could provide the funds. His response was even more puzzling to me.

The Nugget River government, according to the head of chancery, was going through hard economic times. He added that even the high commission was finding it difficult to meet its financial obligations. Upon further questioning, he told me I would have to wait until the high commission could solicit funds from the scholarship secretariat to send me home. I was in shock upon hearing his answers. I explained our housing problem to him and told him I could not work in Multizone and would love to go back to Nugget River. He told me to make an appointment with him again in a week. I did, and once again, I was in shock to hear that I was on my own. Luba and I got angry and panicked. We knew going back to Dusty Rose was not an option. After serious and careful deliberation, I approached the Kolaland embassy in October for help in contacting Dr. Stanley, a professor in the zoology department at the University of Benhur.

I'd met and made the acquaintance of Dr. Stanley when he spent part of his 1984–1985 sabbatical leave visiting Dr. Twistra in the entomology department at the University of Flatland. Dr. Stanley had found out that my parents were from Kolaland, and he was also aware of my plans to return to Nugget River and occasionally visit my parents. He'd come to Flatland with his wife, Gladys, who had become a friend of Luba's. Luba and I had entertained Dr. Stanley and Gladys on several occasions at our home, and we'd organized a farewell party for them the week before they left for Kolaland. We'd invited several students from Kolaland and Nugget River to the farewell party, and everybody had had a good time. Invitees had brought either a dessert or a meal indigenous to their culture. We'd had food from most of the tribal cultures in Kolaland and Nugget River. Dr. Stanley and Gladys had left Dusty Rose at the end of July. Luba and I had promised to keep in touch with them through correspondence.

I was able to contact Dr. Stanley through the embassy of Kolaland. In my correspondence with him, he understood the predicament I was in. I asked him for help in finding a teaching position either at the University of Benhur or in other universities in Kolaland. Shortly after I sent my letter to Dr. Stanley, we had to vacate the unit at the YMCA and YWCA.

Accommodation at Halfway House

The residence manager at the YMCA and YWCA informed us at the end of our two-week lease that we could not renew our lease. We spoke to the social services department, and they relocated us to another address. Luba and I knew there was something unusual about our new residence the moment we saw it.

The appearance of the building reminded me of a fortified prison. After we unloaded our luggage, a gentleman whom we thought was the residence manager gave us a tour of the inside of the building. We were shocked when we discovered the windows were reinforced with steel bars. Our room had enough space for two single beds. There was a fridge in one corner of the room, and we also had a table and two chairs. We were shown the kitchen where all tenants prepared their meals. The kitchen had two stoves, a toaster and a sink. The manager informed us that tenants arranged among themselves as to what schedule to follow to avoid overcrowding in the kitchen. The bathrooms were located on the ground floor, and tenants also had to share those facilities. The most surprising thing to us was when we learned that all tenants had to leave the keys to their rooms at the front counter whenever they went out, even for a walk. We objected to the latter policy, but since we had nowhere to go and had had a negative experience in searching for an apartment, we decided to go along with leaving our key. Our curiosity about the place was soon put to rest after the third day.

During a conversation with one of our neighbours, we found out the building was emergency housing for families and individuals who needed immediate accommodations. It was also used as a halfway house for freed inmates to enable them to reintegrate into society successfully. He told us he had been released from prison after serving time for arson and theft. He further added he was being rehabilitated before gaining his freedom to live in society again. He had been at the halfway house for 15 days out of his expected three-month stay. He told us that most of the other tenants were on a similar rehabilitation program. However, we also met a family temporarily housed in that building who had lost their house in a fire that had destroyed several other houses on their block. Luba and I became apprehensive about the tenants because we did not know the types of offenses they had been imprisoned for. We were particularly worried about our children and wondered if any of the tenants were child molesters or sexual offenders. Our apprehension was heightened when we discovered that our luggage and fridge were being tampered with when we were not in the complex. We reported the tampering to the front counter and were told management would take steps to make our room safer.

Living at the halfway house was stressful for our family. We felt and were treated as if we were under house arrest. For reasons that later became clear to us, we were followed around town and not allowed to live as freely as we would have loved to. No alcoholic drinks were allowed in the complex, even though Luba and I would have loved wine occasionally for dinner. There was also a 10:00 p.m. curfew, after which all tenants were ordered to turn off all musical equipment and go to bed. We felt restricted and wondered why we'd been put into a halfway house. We became more incensed when we discovered that the front desk was manned by non-uniformed police officers and that our excess luggage was in storage at a nearby police warehouse.

We asked why we were being treated as prisoners but received no tangible explanations. Further inquiry into the types of tenants at the building convinced us that something sinister was being planned against us. Arguments and verbal abuse were frequent among the tenants, and we witnessed a few physical fights. On some occasions, we had to endure rude and unprovoked comments and behaviour. Fearing we might be hurt physically or even killed, we decided to move out. The difficulties we'd had during our search for housing were still fresh in our minds and made it hard for us to move out without having a place to move into.

CHAPTER 7
Assistant Professorship: University of Benhur, Kolaland

In the midst of our predicament, I received a letter from Dr. Stanley informing me that the zoology department at the University of Benhur was willing to offer me a position as assistant professor. The excitement over the news made us forget the difficulties and problems we were having.

I contacted the embassy of Kolaland, as the letter instructed me to, to inquire about the preparations I should make in anticipation of going to work in Kolaland. I also sent Dr. Stanley a telegram to acknowledge receipt of his letter and express my gratitude for his help. I asked him to have the registrar's office at Benhur University send me a formal letter of the appointment. The visa section at the embassy of Kolaland wanted an official document of the appointment in order to grant my family and me on entry visa.

We put our plans of moving out of the halfway house on hold because we knew we were soon going to be out of Multizone. We figured we could minimize our contact with the other tenants if we got up early and spent most of the day away from the halfway house. The latter tactic was expensive because we had to eat out, but we achieved our objective, and more importantly, we had more time to make preparations for our trip to Kolaland.

When the formal letter of the appointment arrived, Luba and I were thrilled. The terms of the appointment and prospects for advancement were excellent. We saw the appointment as an opportunity to reorganize our lives and have successful careers in Kolaland. Dr. Stanley and his wife, Elizabeth, had told us when they were in Dusty Rose that Luba's teaching career would be enhanced at the University of Benhur. They'd informed us there were always vacancies in the teaching field for qualified expatriate teachers. The prospects for advancing my research and teaching career were also good. Part of the employment contract involved the award of tenure based on hard work and dedication. I also liked the section of the contract that dealt with pension and remunerations depending on the years of service rendered.

In terms of my research, I was glad I had a position in an institution located in a vector-borne-disease-endemic region. The World Health Organization had informed me they were more interested in funding field and laboratory research on arthropod vectors of disease in that region of the world. I also saw an opportunity to further my research career and maintain contact with scientists in my area of specialization in other countries. Luba and I knew that if everything worked out, we would have no need or want to leave Kolaland. She and the children were citizens of Multizone, and we knew I could always get a visiting visa whenever we wanted to come to Multizone to visit her parents. Despite those facts, Luba told me she would feel more secure if I had my Multizonian citizenship papers. Her main concerns were the unstable nature and sudden change of political activity and leadership in Kolaland and other surrounding nations. She wanted to be sure we could leave Kolaland as a family in the event of sudden political activities that might threaten our lives or destabilize the country. We discussed her concern. To avoid interrupting our preparations for the trip, we decided to continue with the discussion after we arrived in Kolaland.

The Trip to Kolaland

While waiting for our entry visas from the embassy of Kolaland, we made all the necessary arrangements for our luggage to be shipped to the University of Benhur. We also arranged to have Luba and the children immunized. I declined to be immunized. Prior to leaving Dusty Rose, we discussed our plans with our family doctor, and he advised me not to take any immunization shots. He told me there were problems with my immune system that needed to be treated if possible. We completed all arrangements for our trip to the University of Benhur by the end of November. We spent the two weeks preceding our departure to Socan via Appleton Airport saying goodbye to friends and family and doing some shopping for my family in Kolaland. We departed from Looney Bay International Airport at three o'clock p.m. on December 16, 1985.

The flight to Appleton Airport was aboard a small 20-seater airplane. We experienced no turbulence, and the flight crew was courteous. We arrived at Appleton Airport at about four forty-five p.m., and after going through customs, we walked a short distance to the departure gate for our flight to Socan. It was just nine days before Christmas, and the crowd of passengers at the departure gate was overwhelming. There was a long wait for those checking in luggage and for those who wanted to be placed on the waiting list in case of cancellation. The departure time was 7:30 p.m., but the flight was delayed until 8:30 p.m. to give the check-in counter enough time to process the boarding passes of the more than 300 passengers on the flight. Luba and I took turns waiting in line. We had sandwiches while waiting in line, and Luba took care of the children's dinner. The maximum safe weight the plane could carry had been attained by the time we got to the counter at about 7:20 p.m. The plane could accommodate only our carry-on luggage, and we left most of our luggage behind in storage for transfer to the University of Benhur at a later date.

Except for a couple incidences of slight turbulence, we had a smooth flight across the Atlantic Ocean. The food served during our flight was great. Luba, the children and I had a good time chatting and playing together. The children went to sleep just after eleven o'clock p.m. Luba and I engaged in various discussions, and she teased me whenever I shivered and squeezed her hand as our plane suddenly descended to a lower altitude to avoid turbulent air. I was still scared of flying. The flight was my fourth flight since my first flight from Gondwana. I did everything I could to relax. Luba also helped calm me down. We might have fallen asleep sometime after one o'clock in the morning. We woke up at five o'clock, when the pilot told the cabin to prepare for landing in Kapustan. The stopover was a refreshing one for all the passengers. For me, it marked the first time in eight years I'd stepped on Gondwanian soil. It was the cold season in West Gondwana, and the trees at Kapustan Airport had shed their leaves. The air was a little chilly but still too hot for most of the passengers, including Luba and me. We quickly shed the winter clothing we'd worn before leaving Appleton Airport for more comfortable warm-weather attire. People took off their jackets and coats and changed in the airport restrooms and on the plane. We left Kapustan after six-fifteen for Socan.

Arrival at Kondey International Airport, Socan

Our time of arrival at Kondey International Airport in Socan was delayed for more than 30 minutes. There was a thick fog over the city of Socan, and our plane had to wait for instructions from the control tower as to when it was safe to come in and land. The fog prevented us from having a view of the city from the sky. When we finally landed, most of the passengers clapped their hands and shouted to congratulate the pilots on our safe arrival. The airport at Socan was beautiful. The facilities, except for some bathrooms, were comparable to airports in Upper Contica and Oldomia. I was amazed at the size of the airport. We went through customs without any problems.

Prior to our departure, the embassy of Kolaland in Looney Bay informed the University of Benhur about our itinerary. I had also sent a telegram to Dr. Stanley to inform him of our time of arrival at Socan Airport. We expected personnel from the University of Benhur to pick us up at the airport. My younger sister, Jane, and her husband, Albert, showed up a few minutes after we cleared customs. We had informed them of our time of arrival and had planned to meet at the airport to arrange a suitable time for us to come visit them after we settled in at the University of Benhur. I was excited to see Jane and Albert. It was our first meeting in eight years. Luba and Jane took to each other immediately. Jane hugged her and told me in our local language that Luba was very pretty. She also hugged Naomi and Zevin. Albert also made nice comments about Luba and the children and hugged them.

Jane had put on some weight. She looked more beautiful and radiant. We hugged each other and shed tears of joy. Her husband and I had met when I was a student at the University of Nugget River. He and my elder sister Georgina attended an accounting institute close to Noogle. We shook hands, and he congratulated me on my success at Amicus University and the University of Flatland. Jane's two children were not at the airport. She told me they were fine; her mother-in-law was babysitting them. We realized after about 30 minutes that the people from the University of Benhur were not going to show up. After a brief discussion, Albert and Jane agreed to let us spend the night in their house. Jane asked Luba and the children to come with her in the car they'd brought to the airport. Albert arranged for a chauffeur of one of his taxi services to pick up him, me and our luggage.

We ended up spending a couple days at Jane and Albert's house. The neighbourhood they lived in was not rich but had a few nice and expensive homes. We enjoyed the time we spent playing with Jane's little girl and interacting with their neighbours. For me, it was the first time I'd been back in Kolaland since I was about 12 years old. I was glad to communicate again in my mother tongue. I realized I needed to work on my pronunciation of certain words. Jane pointed out to me that my knowledge of the language was still fine, but I had lost the ability to engage in prolonged conversation without having to resort to using English words. I was not surprised at Jane's comment because except for student parties or social gatherings at Amicus University and the University of Flatland, I'd scarcely spoken our local language in the eight years since I'd left Gondwana. Jane, Albert and their neighbours expressed their dissatisfaction at Naomi and Zevin's inability to speak my mother tongue. They more or less scolded and blamed me for refusing to teach my children about my culture.

Albert's mother even went as far as to suggest I should teach Luba my mother tongue. I promised to do my best to help them learn the language. I knew it would be a futile effort to attempt to give them an explanation or engage in a debate over the language issue. Luba's mother had given me a similar lecture in Flatland. She'd suggested Luba should teach our children her mother tongue. Luba and I would have loved to have our children speak both languages, but time and money were limiting factors. We were too involved in our problems to have time to teach the children our languages. Despite our differences on the language issue, my family got along well with Albert and my sister.

Luba and the children were not used to the cuisine in Kolaland. I had to repeatedly remind them there would be Multizonian cuisine at the University of Benhur. We left Socan for the University of Benhur early in the morning on the third day.

The University of Benhur

Before we left Socan in one of Albert's taxis, I promised Albert I would reimburse him for the fare of the taxi from the airport to his home and also for the trip to the University of Benhur. I made a note of the total cost of both trips and planned to ask the university bursar to refund our expenses on transportation since we'd arrived at Kondey International Airport in Socan. Our journey to the University of Benhur was not as relaxing as I had hoped. I was nervous all the way to the University of Benhur, mainly because of the reckless and dangerous manner in which people drove. We were on a two-lane road that was not well maintained. Potholes littered every inch of the road. I had also never observed the reckless disregard for traffic rules that most of the drivers displayed. There was no respect for speed limits. On a number of occasions, I covered my face with both hands when I thought we were going to collide head-on with oncoming vehicles trying to overtake other vehicles at senseless and blinding speeds. The sides of the roads were littered with cars and buses that had either been involved in collisions or had mechanical problems and been looted when the owner went to get help. Our driver told me it was unwise to leave a vehicle unattended on those roads. The scarcity of spare parts made unattended vehicles easy targets for thieves who made their living by pilfering and selling parts from such vehicles. Thank God we made it to the University of Benhur safely after about five hours of tension-filled driving.

Security guards delayed us briefly at the entrance to the campus. They verified I was a new member of staff in the zoology department and did a quick search of our car to ensure we had no firearms on board. Kolaland had just experienced its sixth military coup d'état the day before we arrived in Socan. We'd learned about the military takeover of the democratically elected government at Socan Airport. There were soldiers all over the place at the airport. Security measures were taken to ensure the success of the military takeover. The military authorities were guarding against the threat of counter-revolutionary elements or even forces from outside the country being recruited to topple the coup leaders. Some of those measures were also in effect at the University of Benhur. They let us go when they found no firearms.

Our first order of business was to try to locate Dr. Stanley. As we drove around, we noticed that except for some faculty members and their families, most of the campus was quiet. The university was closed during Christmas break. Most of the students were away, and we learned when we finally located his house that Dr. Stanley and his family were away in Socan on a short vacation. Unlike at most Upper Contican colleges and universities, faculty members at West Gondwanian colleges and universities resided on campus in houses owned by the institutions. Rent for the houses was paid by a minimal deduction from their salaries. As Dr. Stanley was a tenured full professor, his residence was bigger than those of lower-ranked faculty members. We were not allowed access to their house because Dr. Stanley had not informed the caretaker to expect us. We ended up spending the night in the conference centre on campus.

Our accommodations at the conference centre consisted of a small room with a table, two chairs, two beds and a radio with only the campus channel. The four of us felt crowded, but we managed to have a good sleep, perhaps because we were tired from the five-hour journey. The chauffeur stayed overnight in another room and left early the next morning for Socan.

We learned at breakfast that Dr. Stanley and his family had returned from their Socan vacation after we went to bed. Breakfast was at the faculty lounge, which was located a few metres away from the conference centre. Contrary to my family's expectations and all the promises I had made about Multizonian food on campus, the menu was typical Kolalandian fare. I found it difficult to handle the food. I had not had that type of food in eight years, and I found it difficult to eat. Luba went to the kitchen to see if they had milk and bread for the children and her. She returned with some bread but no milk. The cook informed her they had run out of milk and would not be getting any for a while. I looked into Luba's face and knew immediately she was not happy. We decided to go to Dr. Stanley's house to get some milk for the children.

They were glad to see us and told us they'd found my telegram in their mail when they got home the previous night. They had been away on vacation for about a month. My telegram had arrived while they were on vacation. Luba and I found out they didn't have any milk either. Gladys, Dr. Stanley's wife, told us milk was a scarce commodity. She added that they received milk only when it was supplied to the faculty grocery shop. We found out later that all other essential commodities and food items, such as cheese, soap, meat and fish, came through the faculty shop. After lunch, Dr. Stanley came by and gave me a ride to the zoology department. He introduced me to most of the faculty who either had not gone on vacation or had returned from one.

The department was spacious. The faculty offices were large, and their laboratories were well equipped. I was glad to see that the problems we had with accommodations and food were not going to extend to the academic aspect of life at the university. Dr. Stanley did not show me my office and laboratory space. He told me space would be provided for me after some rearrangement and reorganization by technicians and support staff when they returned from vacation before the university resumed. We discussed arrangements for better accommodations for my family on our way back from the zoology department.

One of the terms of the contract I'd signed allowed my family and me to reside in a hotel for a couple weeks to enable the university to locate suitable accommodations for us on campus. I mentioned the lack of space in the room we'd spent the night in to Dr. Stanley, and he promised to try to get us moved into a more spacious room until arrangements could be made for us to move into either our residence on campus or a hotel.

I observed that Luba and the children barely ate their dinner. I was disappointed in the food that was served. The university had faculty, staff and students from abroad. I'd assumed the kitchen made provisions for the foreigners in their daily menu planning. I knew at breakfast the following morning that we would have problems with the children's diet unless another menu was available. In addition to not having a good night's sleep, the children complained of hunger. They had not eaten a decent meal in two days, and I could tell Luba was also feeling pangs of hunger. There were other Upper Contica and Oldomia visitors on campus who informed us we should have brought food with us at least to feed ourselves for the first week. One of them noticed the children looked sick, and he was kind enough to give us a few packages of Campbell's chicken noodle soup. He was a Grandonian tourist who had been in Kolaland for a few months. He explained to us that we should make arrangements to have food and other essential items sent to us from Multizone. We found out from the Multizonian wife of one of the professors in the botany department that was how she had managed to remain in Kolaland. The alternative was to learn to make do with the native diet and improvise for other items, including feminine sanitation items and medicine. She told us about her biannual trips to Multizone to stock up on food and other items. She also brought back items to sell to the wives and relatives of other professors on campus. We thanked her for her advice and planned to engage in a similar type of business once we settled in our home at the university.

The Campbell's chicken soup sustained us for three days. However, we still had neither been given residence on campus nor moved into a hotel. Our luggage had not arrived, and we soon ran out of clean clothes. Without any washing machines, I hand-washed all our dirty clothes and Zevin's dirty diapers. It appeared we were going to have to make do with the small room at the conference centre. I approached Dr. Stanley and asked for arrangements to be made for my family to go spend some time with my parents in Yarntown. We reasoned that by the time we returned from Yarntown, the university authorities would have made suitable arrangements for our accommodations on campus. Dr. Stanley was able to make arrangements for us to be driven in one of the department's vans to Yarntown.

Reunion with the Rest of My Family

The trip to Yarntown was reminiscent of our trip to the University of Benhur. That time around, the drivers were even more reckless and careless. Our driver swore several times in the local language at the manner in which some drivers neglected traffic rules and drove as if they owned the roads. We passed through Throne, my parents' hometown, on our way to Yarntown. I observed that Throne was more cosmopolitan than Benhur. The roads were well maintained and marked. They were dotted in a few places with small potholes. The buildings were cleaner and more modern. I had no memory of what it had looked like when I visited with my dad as a 12-year-old. The downtown core was well organized. Shops lined both sides of the streets. Vendors of different goods were spaced and intertwined among the shops in most areas. I also noticed a few buildings that were 8 and 10 stories high. The driver told me the tall buildings were government offices. We did not have time to stop to look around the town. I knew there would be ample time and opportunity to visit my relatives after we got settled in Benhur. We had little trouble locating my parents' house when we arrived at Yarntown.

My younger brother, Timothy, worked as an assistant technician in the physics department at the University of Benhur. We stopped by his department at the university, and he led us to the house. The sight of Timothy after eight years was beyond description. He ran to me while shouting, "Brother, brother, brother!" We hugged, and he almost lifted me off my feet. He had grown into a strong, big man compared to when I'd left Gondwana. His voice was deep, signaling that the arms of puberty had an initiating influence on him. He was surprised to see us and told me they had not expected us until after the end of December. He then turned his attention to Luba and the children. Luba and Timothy had corresponded on a number of occasions. He hugged her and teased me in our language by saying, "Beauty and the beast." Then he picked the children up one at a time. He held on to Zevin and kept singing to him. After obtaining permission from his immediate supervisor to take the rest of the day off, he led us to the house he shared with Mom and Dad.

Timothy led the way into the house after we unloaded our luggage from the van. I was the last one to enter. I heard my mom ask Timothy, "Why are you home early?" She realized before completing the sentence that Timothy was not alone. "Who is the white lady behind you?" she added. I walked in with Naomi and Zevin before Timothy could answer her question. "My God!" she shouted when she saw me. Without any further delay, she dropped the scarf she was holding and picked Zevin up. She then danced around the seating room. My dad rushed out from one of the two bedrooms to investigate what the commotion was about. He was dumbfounded when he saw me. He waited for a few seconds to recuperate from the shock of the surprise, and then he ran to me and hugged me. The hug lasted for a few minutes because he saw Naomi and immediately let go of me to pick her up. Luba stood by and smiled at all the jubilation going on. Timothy and Luba engaged in a short conversation. My mom and dad were still carrying our children as they came to Luba and hugged her. Then there were a few minutes of silence during which my parents, Timothy, Luba and I shed tears of joy. After everyone settled down, we told my parents about the reasons we had come to visit them earlier than scheduled. They had known we were coming to the University of Benhur, but we were not supposed to visit them until after New Year's. They told us it was a good thing we'd come earlier, because my mom had been getting impatient about having to wait until January 1986 to see us.

We stayed up late that night, catching up on the events of the past eight years. Most of the discussion shifted between events that had happened in the family and my experiences in Multizone. My nephew who also stayed with my parents, came home later that evening. He was excited to see us. He'd been about 9 years old when I left for Multizone. He played with our children for most of the evening. He also engaged in conversation with Luba and me. May he rest in peace. I was not able to go to his burial and funeral. I miss him dearly. His mom, my elder sister, also passed away recently. Sadly, I also missed her burial and funeral. She was the second of my three elder sisters. Her death left another void in my circle of close relatives. Rest in peace, Emilia.

In the morning, my nephew was sent to Brimville to inform my third elder sister, Georgina, of our arrival. Georgina was an accountant in one of the Kolaland banks in Brimville. She knew we were coming to the University of Benhur, but she was not aware we had rescheduled our time of arrival. I had sent her a telegram when we were in Looney Bay to inform her of my appointment with the University of Benhur. At the time I sent the telegram, we thought we were not going to be at the University of Benhur until January 1986, just before the beginning of the second semester.

We spent a good part of our second day at my parents' house resting and talking about Multizone. Most of the discussion centered on Luba and the two children. Everyone wanted to know how we'd met and if the children could speak our local language. There were also a few questions about Luba's family in Multizone. We had sent them pictures of Luba's parents and sisters. My mom in particular was curious about how receptive Luba's parents were to our marriage. She had a nephew whose marriage to an English woman had ended up in divorce. The lack of support from the English woman's family, due mostly to the mixed nature of the marriage, had contributed to the divorce. I told her of the problems we'd had with Luba's parents initially and added that we had been able to work out our differences. She was glad to know we had the support of Luba's parents. More importantly, she told me, Luba was different from her nephew's wife. The English lady, according to my mom, had refused to lodge in the house when they visited Kolaland. She also had complained about the food and been disrespectful to her husband's relatives. During the course of our conversation, I noticed that my dad constantly blinked and rubbed his right eye. I asked him after dinner if he was having problems with his eyes. He wanted to know why I asked the question, and I told him what I'd observed earlier in the day. After a brief pause, he looked at me and said, "I have been feeling some irritation in both eyes, and the right one in particular gets very painful and red occasionally."

In response to my question on when he'd started having his eye problems, he told me the problems had started a few months after he'd had his appendix removed at the hospital in Socan. I had not told my parents about my eye problems, but I was amazed at the similarity between the symptoms of my dad's eye problems and mine. I debated in my mind if I should let my family know I was having eye problems similar to my dad's. After pondering the thought, I decided to wait until Georgina arrived from Brimville to discuss my observations with her. Timothy might have overheard the discussion between my dad and me. He came over to me the next day and told me my dad had not told me about the other problem with his right eye. I asked him what other problem Dad's eyes had. He made me promise not to let Dad know he'd told me. He proceeded to inform me that Dad's vision in the right eye was blurry, and all attempts by doctors to treat the eye had been unsuccessful. I asked Timothy if he knew anything about the treatment Dad had received and what types of medication he was using. He answered both questions in the affirmative.

He gave me a brief description of the information the doctors had told Dad. He also told me the frequency of Dad's visit to the doctor for treatment. He managed to secretly show me Dad's eye medication. The medication was a droplet I was not familiar with. I read the contents of the medicine. It was not an anti-inflammatory steroid or a pressure-lowering medication. I decided to refrain from making any comment or having my dad try my eye droplets until after I had talked to Georgina. I became impatient for Georgina to arrive because of the questions I could not wait to ask her.

The foremost irritant was my inability to wait to find out from her about the doctor and the hospital where Dad had had his appendectomy. She'd made the arrangements for the surgery and accompanied Dad to the hospital. I could tell from listening to Dad and also from the symptoms of his eye problems that he would benefit from using my eye droplets. Waiting to either get him to use mine or talk to his doctor about giving him prescriptions for my type of droplets almost drove me nuts. I became impatient with everybody, including my mom. She noticed that something was bothering me, but I declined to share my thoughts with her because I did not want her to be scared and worried. I did assure her it was nothing serious and said I would talk to her after Georgina arrived from Brimville.

My nephew and Georgina took a day longer than the four days my parents had predicted to make it to Yarntown. She was excited to see us. She quickly made the acquaintance of Luba and the children and told me how blessed I was to have met Luba. I guessed that she and Luba might have talked about me in many of their letters. They wrote to each other several times before they met. The long train journey had made Georgina and my nephew so tired that they withdrew to bed soon after dinner. The rest of us watched TV for most of the rest of the evening. I had my long-awaited talk with Georgina soon after breakfast the following morning. Our talk made Luba and I reschedule our plans to have a meeting with Georgina and Timothy to discuss how to get the rest of my sisters to my parents' house for a family reunion.

Georgina confirmed most of the statements Timothy had told me about Dad's eye problems. She also told me Dad's surgery had been performed at the General Hospital in Socan when he'd gone to visit Jane and Albert. However, she could not remember the name of the surgeon who'd performed the surgery. We talked about his medication, and I elaborated on my eye problems to her. She knew from my letters that I had problems with my right eye and was surprised by the similarity between Dad's and my symptoms. She had no objection to having Dad try my eye droplets, but the problem we had was how to convince Dad to try my medication. Georgina told me to leave the latter problem to her. We agreed to keep the discussion between us until after we saw the results of my medication on Dad's eyes.

Georgina was able to convince our dad to try my medication. She told me she was honest with him about my eye problems and told him my medications had helped me control the pain in my right eye. I was happy about the news from Georgina, but I was worried my dad would inform my mom about my eye problems and get her worried. Georgina told me not to worry about Mom because Dad had given his word he would keep things under the lid until Georgina and I told the family about my eye problems at our family reunion. I had not planned on telling my parents or brother and sisters apart from Georgina about my eye problems. My dad's eye problems, however, gave me no choice but to let them know. Georgina and I, after serious deliberation, came to the conclusion that it was fine to openly talk about Dad's and my eye problems. The question Georgina and I pondered was whether it could be an inherited genetic disease in the family. Thus, we owed it to the other family members to inform them about it. Despite the similarity in symptoms, I doubted the eye problem was a hereditary condition in my family. I knew that none of my dad's relatives had had such an eye problem. In fact, nobody from either my mom's or dad's side of the family or their children had that eye problem. I also found the timing of the onset of both my dad's and my eye problems suspicious. He and I had been in hospital about one month apart, and we both had developed problems in our right eyes. I did not share my suspicions and doubt with Georgina, Luba or anyone in the family. My most urgent objective at that time was to relieve my dad's pain. I knew how painful it was when the eye got inflamed, and I could not imagine how he dealt with the pain without proper medication.

Georgina and I administered my eye droplets into Dad's eye just after lunch. We were careful that nobody in the family saw us or knew about what we had done. We repeated the treatment of 1 percent prednisolone and Betagan, which regulated the eye pressure, in the evening. The next day, we again gave him two drops of each medication three times: after breakfast, lunch and dinner. In the interim, Georgina and I called Jane, Margie, Angela and our two elder sisters and invited them to my parents' house for a family reunion.

We waited for four days before we asked Dad if he had noticed any change in his right eye. Even without asking him, I could tell the right eye had greatly improved. I noticed after the second day of treatment that he stopped rubbing the eye, and the blinking had stopped. In response to our questions, he told us the irritation in the eye had stopped, and the intense sensitivity to bright light, which I had also complained about, had stopped. He was happy about the treatment. The droplets also reduced the pain in his right eye to the point where he could barely feel any more pain. He told us that the time I'd noticed him blinking and rubbing his right eye, he'd been feeling pain in it. He thanked Georgina and me and asked if we could help him get his own supply of the droplets. Fortunately for him, I had extra supplies of my eye medications with me. I knew that as a professor, it might be possible for me to get the medication in Kolaland, although it would probably be too expensive to afford on the salary I was going to receive. My best chance of getting regular supplies would be through a hospital in Big Park, Derkland. I had planned to visit Big Park soon after settling in Benhur to make arrangements for the eye medications.

I gave my dad a bottle of both medications and told him I would supply him with more whenever he needed it. Georgina and I were happy about the positive response of Dad's eye to the medications. To me, it was more proof that my dad and I had, in an inexplicable way, developed the same eye problems at about the same time. The thought of how that could have happened troubled me greatly. I entertained several scenarios that would have made it possible. I had suspected, based on comments made by Drs. Turbulus and Twistra, my eye problems were linked to unauthorized experimentation on me during my knee surgery in January 1983. If my dad had been in the same hospital in Dusty Rose, Flatland, then it would have been possible that whatever had been done to me had been done to my dad also. But he'd been in Kolaland, thousands of miles away from Multizone. My dad had had surgery in Kolaland about two months after my knee surgery. We'd been in hospital at about the same time. Was it possible we could have developed similar postsurgery infections? Could we have been exposed to similar infectious organisms? The scenarios seemed too far-fetched to make any sense to me at that time. Nevertheless, I had an insatiable feeling that the similarity between my dad's and my eye problems was not an act of chance. The odds against the similarity being a chance event were so great that I decided to pursue every lead that would help me find the cause of the problem in his and my right eyes. In the interim, I was happy he had medication to control the inflammation and subsequent pain in the eye. After observing the improvement in Dad's eye, Georgina promised to have a discussion with my dad's doctor to explore the possibility of getting him the types of eye droplets I had given him. The improvement in his right eye was evident during our family reunion.

Within a day of our contacting our siblings, all eight of us, along with the wives, husbands and children of my two elder sisters, were once again together at our parents' home after 15 years. The last time we'd all been together had been in 1970, just before the government of Nugget River expelled all aliens, legal and illegal, from Nugget River. The reunion was great. In all, we had 22 people. We talked about life as children growing up in Natamia, Nugget River. Most of our discussion dealt with the events that had transpired in our individual lives since we'd parted company. The discussion about Dad's and my eye issues was only among the adults.

My mom had mixed feelings when she finally learned the truth about my eye. She was, on the one hand, sad I had developed eye problems similar to Dad's. On the other hand, she rejoiced that my eye medication would relieve the pain in Dad's eye. For the first time, she confessed that Dad's eye, especially the pain, bothered her, and she was disturbed by the thought that he might become blind in both eyes. We reassured her the medications would control, though not cure, the eye problem. We also told her not to worry about Dad or me becoming blind in both eyes. My two elder sisters were not glad when they learned about my family's accommodations and food problems at the University of Benhur, but everybody was glad I had been offered a position at such a good university.

The issue of teaching Luba and our children the local language came up again at our reunion. This time, I informed them that Luba's parents would also like our children to speak their language. Luba and I told them it would be too demanding for the children to learn both languages. I also told them Luba and I had decided to let the children make their own minds up about the languages they wanted to learn later in life. "Luba," I added, "might learn our local language if we stay in Kolaland, depending on what happens when we return to Benhur." My parents wanted to know the conditions under which we would not stay in Benhur.

Luba and I told them we were worried the university authorities might renege on the terms of the contract I'd signed. We informed them we were concerned about my health and would have to go back to Multizone because I could get better treatment there. My mom immediately agreed with what we planned to do. She implored us to invite Dad to Multizone for his right eye to be treated if we ended up going back. Georgina and our two elder sisters took some time to think about the possibility of our going back to Multizone. After dinner, the three of them told us they agreed with Mom's suggestion. Jane and Albert were the only two who tried to encourage us not to go back. Albert studied accounting in Big Park, Derkland, and was aware of the excellent medical facilities available. He suggested I could travel to Big Park for treatment if it became necessary. After careful deliberation, I informed them we would return to Multizone if my health deteriorated and if the University of Benhur did not honour the terms of my contract. I promised to look into Albert's suggestion and to do all I could to stay at the University of Benhur if that were possible.

We stayed at my parents' place for three more days after the reunion. I was glad to see Dad's eyes improve. During the time we were in Yarntown, he had no inflammation or pain in his right eye, and he had no adverse reaction to the eye medications. He was concerned about my chances of getting a job comparable to the one at the University of Benhur if we should go back. I told him not to worry. I even promised to try to send him a couple used cars to enable him to start a taxi business. Before leaving Yarntown, we gave my family most of the items we'd brought with us, including towels, shoes and all the Grandonian currency we had on us. They were grateful for the items and money. We promised to inform them of our final decision on whether to stay or return to Multizone after we returned to the University of Benhur.

The Trip Back to the University of Benhur and Breach of Contract

Our trip back to the University of Benhur was a repeat of the type of driving we had experienced on our two previous trips in Kolaland. I wondered if I would ever get used to the style of driving in that part of Kolaland and if Luba and I would be bold enough to drive on those dangerous roads.

The University of Benhur was still on Christmas break when we got back to the campus. We waited until the next day to thank Dr. Stanley for arranging the trip to Yarntown and to inquire about the progress he had made on getting us better accommodations. We also wanted to find out from him if our luggage we'd left at Appleton Airport had been delivered to the department of zoology at the university. Luba and I were surprised to learn he had been unable to get us any hotel off campus or a bigger room at the conference centre. We were also disappointed to learn our luggage had not been delivered. He told us he was still working on getting us accommodations on campus. His aim was to get us settled on campus before the bulk of our luggage was delivered to us. When I went to the zoology department the following day, I also found out that neither an office nor laboratory space had been assigned to me. The worst problem that made Luba and me make up our minds to leave occurred when Naomi became ill one evening.

She developed a high fever after dinner one evening. We rushed her to the infirmary on campus. We were shocked by the level of sanitation we observed. In an attempt to lower her body temperature, a couple female nurses were to pour cold water on her in a bathtub. The tub they were going to place Naomi in was dirty, and the stench in the bathroom was awful. I raised an objection to putting Naomi in the dirty tub. We decided I'd hold her in my hands while they doused her with the cold water. The most shocking aspect of her treatment was that the pharmacy on campus did not carry the medication the attending physician had prescribed for her. We were told to go to a pharmacy and purchase the medication ourselves. Naomi needed to take the medication immediately to control her fever. There was no bus service between the university campus and downtown. After my running around frantically for almost an hour looking for a ride downtown, one of the professors came to our aid and drove us downtown to the pharmacy.

We were patient until Naomi's condition improved. Then I approached Dr. Stanley and told him about my impatience and frustration with the housing problem and my lack of office and laboratory space. We had also run low on money, so I asked for an advance on my first pay cheque to enable us to purchase food for the children, who had stopped eating the food served in the faculty lounge. Our experience of having to go from door to door to solicit a ride to purchase Naomi's medication made me ask him about the part of my contract that dealt with automobile purchasing allowance. His response to my questions was not encouraging. He told me I had to learn to be patient and wait until after the Christmas break. Luba and I were surprised that no arrangements whatsoever had been made in anticipation of our arrival. We knew that waiting another two weeks for the university to reopen would be too stressful for us to bear, especially the children.

We approached the university bursar and discussed our financial situation with him. He was not helpful when we mentioned to him that I wanted part of my salary paid to enable us to feed the children. We talked to a professor from Allemagnia whom we ran into in the faculty lounge about our problems. He told us he'd had a similar experience when he was recruited. He'd had to wait for six months for housing on campus. His automobile purchasing allowance still had not been given to him after two years. We found out from him that contrary to what was written in the contract, the automobile purchasing allowance was given to senior lecturers and full professors only. He'd been hired as a lecturer, just as I had. He would be qualified for the allowance only after at least four years of teaching and publishing. He also told us there were times when salaries were delayed for up to a month.

We had already made up our minds to leave after the incident with Naomi. The Allemagnian professor's stories opened our eyes to the difficulties associated with life as a junior professor at the University of Benhur. Prior to talking with him, I had suspected the university would not honour my contract when we returned from visiting my parents, and now we had confirmation. I also started having more problems with my eyes and lymph nodes. Luba and I had a lengthy and detailed discussion about all we had observed. After weighing all our options, we decided to return to Multizone at the end of December 1985.

I informed Dr. Stanley of our decision the day after Luba and I made up our minds. He tried to convince me to stay. He suggested I let Luba and the children go back to Multizone and return to join me in Benhur after the accommodation and office space problems were resolved. His suggestion made a lot of sense, but I knew it was not going to be easy to be separated from Luba and the children. I did not like the idea of not seeing Luba and the children for a long time. It was even possible we might not see each other again. I knew Luba would have to go back on social assistance in Multizone. Both she and I hated been given handouts. The salary I would be getting from the university would not make it possible for me to visit or pay their fares, even if the university was able to provide decent accommodations and an office space for me. It was obvious the crumbs she would receive from welfare would not be enough to enable her to take good care of the children, let alone be able to pay for airfare for the three of them. The most important reasons I turned down Dr. Stanley's suggestion were my deteriorating health and unresolved immigration problem. Without resolving the latter problem, I was not sure I would be able to visit my family in Multizone even if I were able to save up enough money. I knew the immigration authorities in Multizone would use my health issue to deny me entry.

Dr. Stanley was not happy when I told him the day after our discussion that I did not want to stay without my family. Until that time, I had not told him about my health problems. I thought it was time for him to know about my eye and lymph node problems, especially since my health was a major reason I was choosing not to stay at the University of Benhur. He sympathized with me, but I could tell from his behaviour that he was not surprised by my revelation. He had asked me the cause of the droopiness of my right eyelid when he saw me in Multizone. I'd told him I had an infection in the eye and hoped to get the infection treated. The droopiness was still noticeable in Kolaland, but he made no comments about my eye until I told him about it again.

My guess was that Dr. Twistra, whom he'd visited in the entomology department in Dusty Rose, might have told him about my eye problems. Dr. Stanley tried to get one of the professors in the ophthalmology department at the University of Benhur to treat and, if need be, operate on my right eye. I declined his offer. I was not sure at that time if I wanted anyone to treat the eye. The doctors in Multizone had not nailed down the cause of my eye and lymph node problems. I didn't want to complicate my problems by subjecting myself to any form of surgery. In a sense, I guess I still could not trust being put to sleep and operated on again. I was afraid I might develop more problems, as I had after my knee surgery in January 1983. We left the University of Benhur on December 28, 1985, for Jane and Albert's house in Socan.

CHAPTER 8
The Journey Back to Multizone

My sister and Albert were disappointed we could not resolve our problems with the University of Benhur. They tried to convince us to try to work things out with the authorities in Benhur. We spent the night at their house, and they drove us to the Multizonian embassy in the morning. We ended up at the Multizonian embassy because we had no money to purchase our return tickets. The University of Benhur was still on Christmas vacation, and our attempts to get the bursar in the accounts department to buy our return tickets were not successful. The bursar told us he could not do anything for us until after the university reopened in January 1986. We tried to borrow money from Dr. Stanley and the bursar but were not successful. I guess they either did not have the amount of money we wanted or could not trust us to deposit the repayment of the loan into their accounts in Grandonia.

We did not have to wait long to see one of the embassy officials after we told the receptionist our reasons for coming to the embassy. The embassy officials told us they would not be able to pay for our airfare, but we could use their phone to contact family in Multizone for help. I called my in-laws, and they agreed to pay for our fare. The officials at the Multizonian embassy in Socan made the necessary travel arrangements for us to return to Multizone after they received confirmation that Luba's parents had deposited the airfare in a Multizonian government account in Multizone.

Our itinerary was the same as when we'd come to Kolaland, but this time around, we were travelling in the opposite direction. We ran into a problem with my immigration status when making arrangements for our stopover at Appleton Airport and for the connecting flight to Passion Flower International Airport in Multizone. My minister's permit to remain in Multizone was valid until June 1986. The Grandonian consulate in Socan refused to issue me a transit visa because the minister's permit was not acceptable to them. Officials at the Multizonian embassy in Socan tried to change our itinerary and have us go to Big Park, Derkland, to Multizone, but their efforts were not successful. Our departure was delayed for one day. Eventually, officials at the Grandonian consulate and Multizonian embassy worked out an agreement that allowed me to stop over at Appleton Airport under Grandonian security escort until our plane left for Multizone. I did not like the arrangement of being escorted through Appleton Airport by Grandonian security, but that was the best solution to my problem. They escorted me through customs, handed my passport over to the Multizonian airplane pilot and kept watch over the plane until we were airborne. I was told the Grandonian consulate officials were suspicious I intended to remain in Grandonia because I had a permit that only allowed me to stay in Multizone until June 1986. The Multizonian pilot handed my passport over to me after we entered Multizonian air space.

The Trip Back to Dusty Rose

At the airport in Luxville, Luba and I had to make the decision to either stay in Luxville or continue to Dusty Rose, Flatland. Luba's parents had deposited enough money to enable us to fly to Dusty Rose. There were several flights to Dusty Rose that day. We knew we had at least six hours to make up our minds regarding what we wanted to do and still be able to catch the last plane to Dusty Rose. After a lengthy period of deliberation, Luba and I decided to call my former supervisor, Dr. Howard, at the Sunnydale campus of Amicus University. We wanted to spend the night at his place and ask for his advice on whether to proceed to Dusty Rose. Several calls later, we gave up on him because nobody answered the phone. We guessed he and his family might have been on vacation, because the Sunnydale campus was still on vacation. We tried calling Dr. Godfather in Looney Bay, but nobody answered our calls after several trials. We could have stayed on the East Coast, but we did not want to be thrown into a halfway house again and be given welfare. Another reason we decided against staying on the East Coast was my health. I wanted to go back to Dusty Rose to see my family doctor and the other specialists from whom I had received treatment. My right eye had deteriorated to the point where I needed to see an ophthalmologist as soon as possible. I knew I could not wait for my files to be transferred from Dusty Rose to an ophthalmologist on the East Coast. We were also in favour of moving back to Dusty Rose because Luba's parents had promised to let us stay in their house until we found our own place. Having made up our minds, we had our tickets validated for our trip to Dusty Rose. While waiting for our flight, we engaged in conversation with several of the passengers on the weather and the availability of employment in the West, especially in Dusty Rose. Any lingering doubts about our decision to go back to Dusty Rose were quickly erased by the encouragement we received from one of the male passengers. He told us that the western region was going through an economic boom. He added that he had met several other people who were relocating to the western region of Multizone to fill new job positions. He encouraged us to go back when we told him about the types of jobs we were interested in.

We arrived at Dusty Rose International Airport at around seven-fifteen p.m., and Luba's parents were there to pick us up. It felt kind of funny and strange to be back in Dusty Rose. A part of me wanted to go back to the East Coast. I kept asking myself why I'd come back to a city that had left me with nothing but bitter memories. Those thoughts and the feeling of what the future had in store for my family and me troubled me. We went to bed late on our first evening at Luba's parents' house because her parents and her elder sister's family wanted to hear about our brief trip to Kolaland. While at their house, we made arrangements to have our luggage, which was in storage in Looney Bay, transported back to Dusty Rose. We discovered after we came back from Kolaland that the plans we'd made to have our things shipped to us in Kolaland had been neglected. The embassy of Kolaland in Looney Bay informed us they'd never received the go-ahead order from the university authorities in Benhur to send our luggage. We ended up staying at Luba's parents' house for a month because of the problems we encountered in getting

Chapter 9
Further Medical Treatment

By the time our luggage arrived in Dusty Rose, I had made an appointment to see Dr. Quill, who eventually became our family physician. He made arrangements for me to see Dr. Ulysses, an ophthalmologist, and Dr. Goldberg, an internist. I had received treatment from both doctors before we left for Kolaland. My visit with both doctors confirmed that my right eye needed immediate treatment. Dr. Ulysses administered an intraocular injection of cortisone the day I visited him. He informed me that he might have to operate on the eye if the injections did not stop the deterioration, which was manifesting as loss of sight. I had, at that point in time, lost most of the central vision in the eye. I still had good peripheral vision when the inflammation in the interior part of the eye was under control. Dr. Goldberg took an x-ray of my chest and told me I had nothing to worry about.

Luba and I also arranged, while waiting for our luggage, for our own apartment and for financial assistance through the department of social welfare. We moved into our new unit a few days prior to our luggage being delivered. We had a spacious three-bedroom unit in a low-rent area on the south side of Dusty Rose. Our apartment was the end unit. We loved it because we had a spacious, unfenced field at the side. We played baseball and other games with our children on the field. I spent most of the year visiting Drs. Goldberg and Ulysses and getting my thesis ready for publication. Despite Dr. Ulysses's treatment of my eye, I continued to lose sight in the right eye. The peripheral vision that enabled me to partially use my right eye diminished to the point where Dr. Ulysses finally performed surgery on the eye in September 1986. He extracted the original natural lens and repaired some of the damage done by the persistent and acute inflammation. He informed me after the surgery that the eye was not a candidate for intraocular lens implantation. He further explained that the inflammation was chronic, and I would need to use anti-inflammatory eye drops for as long as I lived. The eye was covered with several layers of bandages after the surgery. There was noticeable swelling all around the eye. I felt severe pain in the eye for more than a week after the surgery. Needless to say, I was devastated by the postsurgery news about my right eye.

Dr. Ulysses tried a special combination of contact lens and glasses after the wound from the surgery healed. Unfortunately, the combination could not match the focusing ability of my left eye. I could see with my right eye alone when my left eye was closed, but the quality of sight was poor. I could not read even large, bold print with the contact lens and glasses combination. The combination lenses made large objects come into better focus, but I still could not decipher fine details, such as the lines on the palms of my hands. I discontinued using the lenses after trying them for a couple months to avoid causing damage to the left eye. I saw two and, at times, more images of the same object when I tried to use my left eye and the lens combination in my right eye.

Being left with one eye was difficult for me to cope with. I have learned to function with only the left eye. I cannot do a lot of things as well as I used to be able to. My depth of field has changed considerably. I cannot play tennis, baseball or Ping-Pong well anymore. Nevertheless, I am glad I can at least see my family, watch my children grow and enjoy the other beautiful things of nature. We had two more children after Zevin: Jael and Marko. I am particularly grateful I can read and write, although devouring and relishing a good book takes longer. I have to rest my left eye often when I engage in the latter two activities. I continue to use anti-inflammatory eye drops to control the inflammation in both eyes.

Correspondence with the Doctors' Control Board of Flatland (March 1986)

I lodged a complaint about the treatment I'd received from Dr. Crulstein with the Doctors' Control Board of Flatland. The chair of the board wrote back to inform me he'd reviewed the case and had asked

Dr. Crulstein to release my medical records and the slides to my family physician. Dr. Crulstein gave us only the records without the slides. He told us the slides were not available. He recommended to my family physician that I be given stronger doses of prednisolone tablets. My family physician disregarded his recommendations and instead referred me to Dr. Abramsen in August 1987.

Dr. Abramsen's complete medical examination, including a lung function test and x-ray examinations, contradicted Dr. Crulstein's diagnosis of sarcoidosis. He also showed that my angiotensin-converting enzyme (ACE) was very low, a finding that mitigated against sarcoid. Further medical examination by Dr. Goldberg supported Dr. Abramsen's findings. Dr. Goldberg instructed me to stop the oral doses of prednisolone prescribed by Dr. Crulstein. He informed Dr. Ulysses, the ophthalmologist, about his findings. After more medical tests and chest x-rays, Drs. Ulysses and Goldberg agreed that 1 percent prednisolone and Betagan should still be used to treat my right eye. Some of the swollen lymph nodes subsequently became normal. My right scalene node and some joints in my fingers are still swollen.

When Dr. Crulstein turned down the request for the biopsy slides, I lodged another complaint with the chair of the board of Doctors' Control Board of Flatland about Dr. Crulstein's action. The chair of the board's response to my letter was not encouraging. He basically told me he had reviewed the case and found nothing wrong with the way Dr. Crulstein had handled my request. I was surprised the chair of the board was not helpful. I wrote him a letter in which I expressed my dissatisfaction with his inability to get Dr. Crulstein to release the slides. I aborted further efforts to obtain the slides because Dr. Goldberg told me he had enough data to support his diagnosis of no sarcoidosis. We discussed the possibility of doing another lymph node biopsy, but Dr. Goldberg consulted with my family doctor, and they decided against it. They felt the blood and urine tests, chest x-ray and lung function test were enough to convince the immigration authorities I was in good health.

CHAPTER 10
Further Search for Employment

Problems with Employment Search

Luba and I had great potential as a high school home economics teacher and a research entomologist, respectively. Over the years, it was difficult for us to obtain gainful and permanent employment.

My visa status did not authorize me to work. Multizonian citizens and other status holders were given priority over people with my type of special permit when vacancies became available. I was informed there were many Multizonian citizens with qualifications similar to mine, and my chances of finding employment with the national government and other employers were virtually non-existent. Prospective employers told me to obtain work authorization from the Multizonian immigration authorities in order to be eligible for job interviews and subsequent employment. There were occasions when I was the most qualified applicant. It was particularly frustrating to be invited to interviews with my former students, who ended up with the positions. I had taught those students the principles and details of the knowledge base in the subject area required for the position. There were a number of occasions when Multizonian agricultural authorities held a position for me pending a work authorization visa from the Multizonian immigration authorities. None of those jobs came to fruition because of the lack of an employment authorization visa.

My wife had the authorization to work. She was a native of Dusty Rose. She was invited to several interviews for teaching and non-teaching positions. She eventually stopped applying for employment when we realized none of her interviews were ever going to be fruitful. She was even turned down for jobs in the retail and restaurant industries. It became obvious to us that there were parties who wanted to keep both of us on social assistance.

Employment Interview: Hope Laboratories in Rich Town

My ceaseless effort to obtain employment resulted in an invitation for an interview in February 1989 for the position of research scientist with Hope Laboratories in Rich Town. In an inexplicable way, Hope Laboratories did not explicitly convey the outcome of the interview to me. They retained me as a consultant from April 1989 to September 1991. I provided advice for improving the formulation of *Bacillus thuringiensis israelensis* (*Bti*).

My contribution helped the company improve the formulation of *Bti* so that the toxic crystal component bonded to a suitable substrate that enhanced the downstream carry of the substrate-toxin complex (particulate insecticide). Downstream carry, or the distance to which a particulate insecticide would travel before the suspended particles would sediment (sink), was an important factor in the formulation and effectiveness of particulate insecticides.

Chapter 11
Medical Lawsuit against Dr. Cutworm

The stressful and unacceptable developments in the employment and immigration scenarios compelled me to file a lawsuit against Dr. Cutworm. I filed the lawsuit in the regional court in Dusty Rose, Flatland, seeking compensation for medical malpractice. After I filed the lawsuit, we received several threatening and racially explicit phone calls. Our house was stoned, and empty beer and wine bottles were smashed on our doorstep. We reported the incidents and threats to the law enforcement authorities in Dusty Rose.

I filed for discontinuance of action on the statement of claim due to the lack of legal representation. All my attempts to retain private legal counsel were fruitless. The lawsuit option became the only viable cause of action when subsequent effort to seek remediation and subsequent compensation failed to produce a satisfactory result. I filed an order for leave to set aside discontinuance of action on the statement of claim. The court rejected the latter application.

CHAPTER 12

Medical Examinations
and Letters to Support
Immigration Application

My family doctor contacted the immigration authorities in Dusty Rose, who told him to attach copies of the medical examinations by Drs. Ulysses, Abramsen and Goldberg to his letter to enable their department to re-evaluate my health. After reviewing the three reports, the immigration authorities asked me to go for another medical examination from one of the immigration doctors. They said it was departmental policy not to accept reports of medical examinations performed by non-immigration-appointed doctors. Dr. Goldberg in particular was incensed by the statement of the immigration authorities. He and my family doctor petitioned the immigration authorities to accept their reports. Their petition mentioned that it would cost thirty-seven dollars per month to buy medication for my eye since that was the only problem with my health. Their petition was turned down. After deliberating on the matter, they told me to go for the medical examination.

The results of my latest medical examination were again sent to Looney Bay for assessment. Unlike the previous result, which had taken a year to assess, the decision of the immigration department was quick that time around. I heard from them within one month, and to my and my doctor's surprise, they said the results were not acceptable to them again. Their reasons were basically the same: "You would be a burden on the health and welfare systems because immigration doctors anticipate your health will deteriorate further with time."

I knew after my second results were rejected that I needed the help of a lawyer. The problem with getting a lawyer was not the lack of good ones but the cost of paying legal fees. Financially, Luba and I were in a tight situation. After my convocation in June, I had no source of income and had to go on public assistance. We discussed our problems with legal-aid authorities. We asked for their help in getting legal representation in our attempt to resolve my immigration medical problems.

Our lawyer reviewed my medical reports from the immigration authorities and those submitted by my family doctor and the other two doctors to whom I was referred. He wrote to the immigration department and requested an explanation for their rejection of the results of my latest medical examination. He received the same response I'd received when my doctors and I had written to them. My lawyer's response also included a paragraph emphasizing the need for me to undergo further treatment because of immigration's concern about the further deterioration of my health. They promised to review my application if future medical examinations satisfied their concern over the possible deterioration of my health.

I sought further legal representation through legal aid. I received legal representation from another immigration law firm in Dusty Rose. I submitted records of new medical examinations by doctors chosen by my lawyers, including the report of Dr. Abramsen to the minister of employment and immigration. My lawyers pleaded that on compassionate and humanitarian grounds, I should be granted a special status immediately so I could obtain employment to support my family. I made several calls to the office of the minister of immigration. I was told the petition from my lawyers and the medical records were under review. In January 1988, upon the recommendation of the office of the minister, immigration authorities provided me with an explanatory letter to present to prospective employers. The letter included the information that I was on a special permit until 1990. I was not aware that all employers associated that type of permit with visitors who were not allowed to work in Multizone.

CHAPTER 13

Protest at Immigration Office in Dusty Rose, Flatland

Luba and I became angry and disappointed with the immigration authorities because of the lack of progress on my application. We found ourselves in a situation that threatened our future plans. We carefully analyzed and debated the outcome of the options we were left with to deal with our unexpected quagmire and the possibility that the immigration application would not be successful. The size of our family had increased to six. We'd had two more children: Jael was born on May 13, 1987, and Marko, her younger brother, was born on March 15, 1989. It became clear to us that the problems I was having with my application to remain in Multizone could split up our family if I went back to Nugget River without the authorization to remain in Multizone. I would have to apply again from Nugget River after my five-year service tenure. We knew it would be impossible to have the application approved when I left for Nugget River. The difficulties we were encountering even while I was in Multizone were an indication that any effort in Nugget River would be foolishness. The quality of treatment and the availability of my eye medications in Nugget River also weighed heavily on our minds.

The least favourable option for my family and me was to stay in Dusty Rose. I wanted to keep some distance between me and the entomology department. I was worried about being hurt by Dr. Turbulus and some of the professors in the department. I knew I could not work with the special permit. The five-year waiting period on social welfare cheques was something Luba and I didn't even want to think or talk about. It was not the lifestyle we envisioned for our family. We finally settled on moving to Looney Bay for two important reasons.

Firstly, our lawyer had suggested we send a petition to the immigration minister in Looney Bay to ask for a review of my application, and Luba and I felt that an appointment with the minister would enhance our chances of getting the minister to intervene in our case. Secondly, we also wanted to go to the high commission of Nugget River to make arrangements for our family to return to Nugget River if our meeting with the minister was not fruitful in resolving our dilemma. Despite our concern over my health and the quality of treatment I would receive in Nugget River, we knew that going back would be better than staying in Multizone on public assistance. I did not want my career to lag behind. I also wanted to contribute to the efforts of the Onchocerciasis Control Program (OCP) in West Gondwana. I was aware the World Health Organization (WHO) was interested in my area of specialization and would approve my applications for research and publication grants. We also considered a plan to relocate to Grandonia, Derkland or Crimson after my service to the government of Nugget River. Our long hours of careful deliberation and thought yielded no satisfactory solution.

My wife and I finally decided to confront the immigration department. We went into the immigration office in Dusty Rose with our four children and refused to remove ourselves from the office until they changed my immigrant status to enable me to work. Our unconventional and desperate action earned us a letter to cross the border at Modez, Flatland, into Grandonia to apply from outside Multizone. Multizonian law did not allow that type of application to be made within the borders of Multizone.

The Trip to Modez: Change of Immigration Status (June 1989)

We departed for Modez the following day. Our preparation for the trip included packing the items our children needed for the trip and a first-aid kit; careful inspection of the car fluids, tire pressure and other necessary items for the trip; and our usual morning family prayer and meditation. We normally recited the Lord's Prayer together to end our morning devotion. Luba and I asked God for travelling mercies and for guidance and protection on our trip as we drove out of our parking lot. Two hours into our journey, I heard a rumbling noise from the front tire on the driver's side. I also noticed the car was veering to the right. I immediately applied the brakes and brought the car to screeching halt on the side of the road. I quickly got out of the car to examine the tire. Luba and the children joined me as fast as they could get out of the car.

The first thing that caught my attention was the angle at which the tire was oriented to the axle. Upon careful examination, I noticed that three of the four bolts that held the tire to the axle were loose. The tire was almost coming off the axle. It was barely held in place by a few threads of the three bolts. We had been lucky. Luba and I looked at each other, shook our heads and breathed sighs of relief. Our family gathered together and gave God praise after we recited Psalm 23. Just as I was going to talk with Luba about the potentially deadly accident we could have been involved in, a truck stopped beside us. A man poked his head out the window, looked at us and told us, "You are lucky. You must be in the right church." The truck driver then drove away without offering us any assistance. My wife and I were baffled by his comment as we watched the truck drive off. Upon second thought, I remembered that the same truck had been behind us about half an hour into our journey. The truck had been visible in the driver's-side mirror. It had not overtaken us when I'd slowed down to enable him to pass us.

Luba and I wondered about what might have happened to the tire. We had not had any work done on the four tires, nor had we changed any tires on the car ourselves prior to embarking on our trip. My careful inspection of the tires the previous day had shown that all four nuts held the tires in place tightly. I was able to elevate the car on a jack and tighten the four bolts. We made it safely to South Town, where we spent the night. The next morning, we inspected all four tires carefully prior to going to a garage to consult with a mechanic about the incident with the tire the previous day.

At the garage, a mechanic hoisted the car up and inspected the axle. He informed me there was nothing wrong with the axle. He could not think of the cause of the loose bolts except that the bolts had not been tightly attached to the axle. He advised me to check the tightness of the

CHAPTER 14

Research Associate Position at Shoreline University, Redberry

My family and I left Multizone in September 1999, when I was offered a research associate position in the department of biology and physiology at Shoreline University in Redberry, Grandonia. We received news of the appointment with great jubilation and thanksgiving. We felt like travellers who'd unexpectedly found an oasis after several days of wandering without water while lost in a vast desert.

Our children were on summer vacation when we received news of the employment on Luba's 40th birthday, August 30, 1999. It was a lovely surprise and a fitting birthday gift for Luba. The good news came at a time when the family needed relief from the status quo. Luba quickly made arrangements to collect the children's academic transcripts from their respective schools. The international students' office and the department of biology at Shoreline University made arrangements with the immigration services office on Shoreline's campus to issue the appropriate employment visa to me. Luba and the children were issued visas that enabled them to work and go to school, respectively. Dr. Gladstone, with whom I was going to do research, found suitable accommodations for us on a bus route to campus a week before we departed for Shoreline University.

I rented a U-Haul truck in addition to our van. We managed to pack our luggage and still have enough room for the six of us. Luba and our two daughters, Naomi and Jael, went in the van. I was accompanied in the U-Haul by our two sons, Zevin and Marko.

We left Multizone on September 26, 1999, and arrived in Redberry on September 29, 1999. It was dark when we made it to Redberry, but we were able to locate our house. Dr. Gladstone had sent me via email good directions to the house a week before our departure date.

I called Dr. Gladstone the next morning and made arrangements to go to the biology department later that morning. It was necessary for me to make it to the department to meet him and get organized for work the next day. I was a week behind schedule due to the delay in issuing our visas.

The meeting with Dr. Gladstone went well. He introduced me to some of the professors and staff. I collected keys to my laboratory and all the other relevant rooms I would be visiting or using. I spent the rest of the morning completing forms and the necessary documents at the international services office, the biology department and immigration services. Dr. Gladstone and I spent most of the afternoon discussing aspects of his research on the interaction of benthic invertebrates with pollution. The discussion helped elucidate the scope and nature of my involvement in the research. I spent the rest of the afternoon familiarizing myself with the campus with the help of a campus map included in the package I'd received at the administration office.

I realized from the campus map that I needed more time than what was left in the afternoon to do a thorough and satisfactory tour of the whole campus. To make good use of my time, I chose the area of campus close to the biological sciences building. A quick and cursory overview of the map indicated the Shoreline campus had bountiful flowers. I noticed that commemorative plaques of Shoreline soldiers who'd fought and made the ultimate sacrifice for their country during the Second World War were cemented under the campus's oak trees. I spent part of the afternoon reading the plaques. I was moved by how young some of the patriots were when they enrolled in the military or were drafted. In an inexplicable way, the time I spent reading the plaques and learning about the ages, sexes, towns and names of the patriots that afternoon developed into a habit later. I used to go to different areas of campus on Saturdays and some Sundays to read plaques and make a mental record of who the patriots were.

My tour took me to the Shoreline basketball sports centre and the football stadium. I had read much about the athletic program at Shoreline University. I knew that one of the National Basketball Association's stars used to play for the Shoreline University basketball team. His contribution and greatness in the NBA made me curious to see where he'd played as a student. The more time I spent visiting various locations on campus, the more aware I became of the beautiful architecture and designs of the buildings. I observed that most of the buildings were made of red-brick blocks and had red-brick roofs reminiscent of the buildings on the campus of the University of Nugget River. I found out later that concrete and brick materials had to be used to protect the buildings against termite damage.

The afternoon went by fast. I would have seen more of the campus on my tour, but I spent most of the time in awe of the beautiful subtropical vegetation and flowers. The vegetation on Shoreline University's campus and most of the landscape in Shoreline was reminiscent of the tropical environment I'd grown up in. I had spent most of my time in Upper Contica in Multizone and in the northern part of Grandonia, except for a brief visit to Kolaland in December 1985. The Shoreline University campus in late summer and early fall had the look, smell and temperature of the University of Nugget River. The odor of beautiful and colourful flowers perfumed the air. It was like the time of year in the tropics when numerous varieties of pollinating, nesting and mating bees, butterflies, wasps, flies, beetles, nuisance vector mosquitoes and colourful singing birds filled the air with buzzing and music. A strange and pleasant memory swept over me as I gazed in awe, amusement and disbelief at the scenery that unfolded before me. I discovered a part of human consciousness that afternoon.

I found out there is a dimension of our consciousness that is awakened when we are in physical surroundings we used to live in. The awareness enables us to reminisce, takes us back in time and opens the channels of our thoughts to pleasant and melancholic events we used to know and feel. To summarize succinctly, I felt and could realize my teenage and early adult years in Nugget River. I felt as if I were back in Nugget River, and I knew then that Shoreline had more for me to discover and enjoy. I made it back home at about five-thirty.

While I was on campus, Luba and the children managed to unload some of our luggage, and they had our mattresses and pillows on the floor in the bedrooms to make sleeping more enjoyable than on the night we'd arrived. We had dinner in a pizza joint close to our house. I spent all of the first weeks getting my laboratory and office ready and unloading the U-Haul truck. We were able to get settled into our home by the end of the second week, thanks mostly to the efforts of Luba and the four children.

Luba made the acquaintance of the wife of the police officer in the house next to ours. Together they made arrangements to have the children registered in school. The police man and I got along well. They had two children. The friendship and the help we received from our next door neighbour contributed immensely to our ability to gradually make a smooth transition culturally and socially to life in Redberry.

The children initially missed their friends and schools in Looney Bay. It took close to a whole semester for them to get used to the academic system in the southern region of Grandonia. They particularly did not like getting up at five-thirty in the morning to get ready to catch the school bus. They also complained bitterly that the academic curricula were not challenging enough. The latter feeling changed when we made arrangements to have them transferred to a more rigorous program in the magnet schools. Although the magnet system was managed by the public school administration, respective students had to score above the normal average to be admitted to the magnet program.

When the children were settled in their schools, Luba spent most of her time decorating and making our house livable. I was busy on campus with administrative and academic arrangements to enable me to be officially capable of getting research done. Another important task I accomplished soon after we arrived was seeing an ophthalmologist. I made arrangements to see Dr. Ford, my new ophthalmologist in Redberry, after we unloaded the U-Haul and got the house in order. During my first visit with Dr. Ford, he performed a careful and prolonged examination of both of my eyes. He asked if I had had any trauma, such as a blow to the eye, or any other event that could have caused the damage to the optic nerve. I informed him that I'd lost sight in the right eye after I had the lens extracted in Looney Bay. He was curious about the nature of the surgery to remove the lens and asked several questions on who had done the lens extraction and how. He told me after hearing my response that the optic nerve in my right eye had been severed, and the retina and other parts of that eye had been damaged beyond repair. He further added that I might need to have the cornea in the left eye replaced because it was thin and had worn out, perhaps because of the prolonged use of steroids and occasional intraocular steroid injections in Multizone.

Research at Shoreline University

I performed research in the department of biology and physiology and the department of entomology when I was at Shoreline University.

Research in the Department of Biology and Physiology

My research with Dr. Gladstone dealt with a species of sludge worm, *Ilyodrilus templetoni* (Haplotaxida; Tubificidae). Our objective was to shed more light on particle size selection, bioavailability and fecal content of polycyclic and polynuclear aromatic hydrocarbons (PAHs) that occurred in the sediment of polluted rivers and streams where the worms were found.

The mass balance approach enabled us to calculate the amount of PAH degraded by the worms using metabolic (enzyme) pathways. We did not investigate the latter pathways. Our results were not conclusive because we lost some of the worms in our replicate samples. I later learned from Dr. Gladstone that replicate portions of the six particle-size fractions of the sediments gave better and more conclusive results when they were autoclaved for about 15 seconds prior to being inoculated with phenanthrene and 14C phenanthrene and then tumbled. He discovered that the bacterial content of the sediment needed to be reduced by autoclaves to prevent the worms from being killed by infection from the bacteria.

In addition to our academic relation and cooperation, Dr. Gladstone's family and mine interacted socially. He invited my family to social activities in his house, which gave Luba and I the opportunity to become better acquainted with other faculty and staff in the biological sciences department.

Dr. Gladstone's wife, played piano and was active in her church's musical programs. I was privileged to play the piano in their home. She invited us to a Christmas musical bells concert she directed at her church. The sound was heavenly. Our children were particularly excited about the concert because it was the first time they'd attended a live musical concert. We had several other occasions to interact and socialize with the Gladstones and other faculty and staff in the department. During our first summer picnic, Dr. Gladstone started the picnic by saying, "Let the good times roll," a phrase commonly used at the beginnings of parties and picnics in the southern region of Grandonia. Indeed, we had a good time, and we also adopted that saying. I wish I could have stayed longer and worked with Dr. Gladstone on the latter part of the research that involved autoclaving. I saw the improved data of the autoclaved sediment size portions. I left his laboratory because I was offered another postdoctoral research position in the entomology department. The biological sciences building housed both departments. I wanted to pursue further research in entomology, and I could not turn down the offer. Prior to my changing departments, Luba's parents told us they were coming to visit us.

Visit by Luba's Parents

Luba's parents came to Shoreline in April 2000 to spend a week with us. Dr. Gladstone gave me permission to be absent from the laboratory until six o'clock in the evening during the visit. Our children were glad to see their grandparents again. We showed them most of the Shoreline University campus and other tourist attractions in Shoreline. We also travelled to Grapevine. Luba's dad was delighted when we went to the harbour in Grapevine. He spent most of the time at the harbour on one of the retired navy warships anchored at the harbour. We purchased tickets to take a tour on one of the warships. The guide took us to the crew's sleeping quarters, the dining room, the captain's room and most of the other rooms on the ship. Luba's dad fell in love with the armoury and the gun turrets. He listened attentively as the tour guide explained the procedures and mechanisms used to engage enemy warships. The warship reminded him of his military service and gave him the opportunity to give us another lecture about his time in the army. We had heard the story countless times, but everybody in our group endured the repetition because we knew how much he valued his service to his country.

The other delightful part of their visit was our trip to a historic site near Grapevine. Historic sites were present in most of southern Grandonia. They were the places where former wealthy farm owners had lived with their farm labourers who'd worked on the acres of farmland. On our tour, we were taken to the farm labourers' cabins. The homes of the wealthy landowners were well furnished and maintained by the labourers. In contrast, the cabins of the labourers were poorly furnished. The historic site we visited was not different from most of the other historic sites. The interesting part of our visit was the historical account of the development and economic value of the historic sites. The stories were sad and unbelievable but true. All of us were grateful to God for the men and women whose consciences could not tolerate the wealthy landowners abusing and taking advantage of the farm labourers and who spoke out against it, even at the cost of their lives.

We spent the rest of Luba's parents' visit at home. We had not seen each other since we relocated to Looney Bay. They were glad to hear that all the grandchildren were enjoying their school activities. The week went by fast. It was difficult to see them go, but we rejoiced that we'd seen each other and learned much about naval warfare and the history of unethical labour practices in the southern part of Grandonia.

Research in the Department of Entomology

While working with Dr. Gladstone, I made time to attend the weekly seminars in the entomology department. I became friends with some of the graduate students and faculty. My visits to the weekly seminars exposed me to most of the research and other entomological programs in the department. With time, most of the students and faculty found out I was an entomologist.

Further interaction with some of the faculty members and my

involvement in the discussions at the seminars led to an offer of employment with Dr. Ziggs. He was an urban entomologist, and his research focused on the ecology and control of native and Formosan termites. I was fortunate to have met and worked with him.

The timing of my employment with Dr. Ziggs couldn't have been better for both of us, more so for me. He needed a replacement for one of his two research assistants, who had to move to another job. I was out of a job at a time of year when relocating back to Multizone would have affected the academic schedule of our children.

The research with Dr. Ziggs dealt with sampling live and dead trees in Grapevine and Lake Philip in Shoreline for native and Formosan termite infestations. The primary objective was to evaluate the post-treatment effect of two termiticides, Termidor and Premise, on the two species of termites.

A major source of funds for the research was a grant from the Shoreline legislature under the Formosan Termite Initiative (FTI) program. Some chemical companies also provided chemicals (termiticides) and minimal funding. The FTI was a multi- regional effort involving most areas of the southern region to manage and control the spread of Formosan termites to neighbouring regions and combat the damage to trees, houses and other structures through intensive research. The report below summarizes my involvement in the FTI.

Native and Formosan subterranean termites have become destructive pest insects affecting trees, houses and other structures in most southern areas. My involvement in the Formosan Termite Initiative (FTI) in Shoreline enriched my experience and knowledge of the ecology and management of structural and forest pest insects.

I was part of the team that examined and identified live trees in Grapevine and Lake Philip for termite infestation in the spring, summer and fall of 2000 and 2001. We used visual and drill-and-scope techniques. The visual technique consisted of physical examination of the exterior of the tree for termites or termite mud tunnels and used a screwdriver to pry and dig for termites. In the drill-and-scope technique, we used a 10-millimetre-wide drill point to make three or five holes, depending on tree diameter, in a live tree until we felt a void spot or until about a foot of drill hole was made. We inserted a tiny, high-resolution digital camera on the end of a specially built electrical coil into the hole to look for termites in the interior part of the tree. A television monitor attached to the other end of the special electrical coil revealed the presence or absence of termites. When needed, we prepared photographic images of the termites from floppy disks using a software package developed by Microsoft Corporation.

The latter technique was more accurate. About 10 to 15 percent of the trees scored as negative with the visual technique were found to have termites. We kept no records of other pest insects, such as beetles, plant bugs and moths, in the interior part of the trees we examined with the scope. It was, however, evident that the scope offered a more accurate technique for detecting and sampling those types of forest pest insects. We observed that fire ants attacked and killed both native and Formosan termites, but using them in a termite IPM program would not have been a good approach because we found out that the ants also damaged most of the trees in which we found termites. The effort to find suitable predatory insects and other organisms that can be used as biological control agents in an IPM program has been initiated by sending scientists to the country, from which the Formosan termites were introduced to Grandonia.

Six-monthly evaluation of post-treatment effects of two termiticides, Termidor and Premise, is ongoing. Preliminary data on treated and control trees indicate that both chemicals are effective in controlling termites in live trees.

We also maintained a laboratory culture of termites in stumps of infested trees cut and brought from the field. Part of our research dealt with the identification of infested tree species. The identification was done by experts in the botany department with the samples of leaves and buds we collected in the field.

I spent the bulk of my time with Dr. Ziggs on the termite research. I also occasionally helped with laboratory work and the collection of ticks from the field. Dr. Ziggs and another postdoctoral fellow collaborated with a professor in the biochemistry department, on the synthesis of a naturally occurring chemical from vetiver grass. To date, they have succeeded in the synthesis of vetiver oil and nootkatone and shown that those chemicals are effective as termite repellents. Nootkatone was also tested on ticks and other urban and medically important arthropods and shown to have potential as a repellant.

My tenure with Dr. Ziggs broadened my knowledge on the importance of termites in forest and urban ecology. Luba and I made time to interact with Dr. Ziggs and his wife, at parties and other social functions in the entomology department and their residence. He was a tireless worker in the field and laboratory. His numerous publications and patents continue to shed substantially more light on the ecology and biology of both Formosan and native termites.

Dr. Ziggs and I had talked about my submitting an application to Grandonian immigration services on campus through the international services office to have my employment visa changed to another class of visa. The latter visa category would enable me to apply to become a citizen of Grandonia after five years. There were several reasons I wanted to change my visa. The most important and valid reason was the availability of permanent employment, especially in the area of termite management and control. In order to apply for those permanent positions, I needed to have the visa that enabled me to become a Grandonian citizen in five years.

My chances of being employed permanently in the area of termite ecology or management and control improved markedly by my making the acquaintance of Dr. Ziggs's associates and other research professors from Long River and Lovelane, and other neighbouring towns who were involved in termite research. Additionally, I also met and interacted with personnel from the pest-control products industry who were involved in the FTI. The latter type of visa would also enhance and benefit our children's education.

Generally, children of people with that type of visa could apply for scholarships and other educational grants. Our children also had the added advantage of applying for several other merit-based minority scholarships and funds. The number of institutions of higher education in Grandonia compared to Multizone also offered our children more choices and chances to pursue their educational goals. We had other worthy reasons for deciding to get that type of visa.

Our desire to reside in Grandonia permanently was also necessitated by the fear of coming back to Multizone to face unemployment and unprovoked harassment and humiliation again. Psychologically, it would be a mental struggle and agony for me to seek treatment for my eye and other health problems in Multizone without the fear of being hurt. The rest of my family also had similar psychological problems concerning going for treatment in Multizone. During the process of making the application to acquire the new type of visa, my eye problems flared up again.

CHAPTER 15
Cornea Transplant at Grapevine University

On October 21, 2001 at about 11:00 p.m. I felt fluid burst out of my left eye. My wife noticed a small hole on the pupil. I was immediately driven by a friend to a hospital in Grapevine where I was seen by the emergency doctor on call. He diagnosed my condition as a corneal rupture and made arrangement for me to have surgery on the eye. The next morning a couple of cornea transplant specialists performed the operation to repair the cornea in the eye. The cornea transplant surgery was not successful.

One of the surgeons who performed the unsuccessful cornea transplant referred me to Dr. Goodkind who was the cornea specialist and department head at the ophthalmology clinic of Grapevine University and Hospital. I learned later that improper suturing procedure had caused the failure of the transplant. Dr. Goodkind performed a careful and more detailed examination on both of my eyes and found out the cornea in my right eye was also in bad shape and could rupture if not fixed.

Dr. Goodkind operated on my right eye on October 31, 2001. He surgically patched the weak portion of the cornea and informed me that the internal damage to my right eye was too severe to enable him to restore sight to that eye. He asked if I'd received a severe blow or been hit by a hard object in the right eye. He looked surprised but said nothing when I told him I had not had any traumatic injury to my right eye. Dr. Goodkind performed the corneal transplant surgery on my left eye on

November 6, 2001. The surgery was successful. I am able to read with the eye by wearing a special soft contact lens that corrects for astigmatism.

I continued to follow up on the activities in Dr. Ziggs's laboratory since I regained sight in my left eye. After the devastation wrought on the levees by a strong hurricane in the summer of 2005, he initiated experiments at the University of Shoreline's agricultural citrus research station at Mander Port. His objective is to evaluate the ability of vetiver grass to protect earthen levees on the open coast. The plant is widely used for erosion control in most parts of the world. Termites are partly to blame for weakening levees by tunneling in earthen levees. The extensive and deep root system of vetiver grass coupled with its repellent chemical properties make the grass an ideal candidate for protecting the earthen levees against termite damage.

CHAPTER 16

The Trip Back to Multizone

I continued to see Dr. Goodkind for follow-up care and treatment until March 30, 2006, when we came back to Multizone. Luba and I, with our eldest child, Naomi, returned to Multizone because our visas had expired. We left Zevin, Jael and Marko behind at the University of Uniontown. The university was still in session, and we did not want to interfere with their academic programs.

Denial of Employment: Back on Welfare

We knew we were back to the same old situation in Multizone within a month of our arrival. A couple of our close friends with whom we used to attend church prior to our departure to Shoreline picked us up at Looney Bay Airport. We spent the first weekend with their family. It was interesting to see each other again, especially their two sons. The boys had grown taller and bigger. They took after their dad's exceptional height. They remembered us and inquired about our other three children. Their family used to live around the corner from us in the same neighbourhood. The boys were close friends of our children. They'd attended and spent much time together in the same Sunday school and church summer camps.

The courteous welcome and assistance from our Christian friends cushioned much of the shock of relocating to Looney Bay. Further help from our friends was instrumental in having the social services department move us into a hotel for one week. We were moved to a familiar emergency shelter: the halfway house where we used to live before we departed to Kolaland. Luba and I had no foreknowledge or information that we were being moved to that address. We stared at each other in open-mouthed bewilderment and broke out into nervous giggles. It was as if we were having a bad dream. A thousand and one thoughts of our previous experiences at that address raced through our mind. We experienced feelings of déjà vu. In an inexplicable way, we were able to suppress our emotions and initial shock and remain calm. Our unit the second time around was in the basement. We'd lived in a third-floor unit during our previous stay. Our second stay at the halfway house was brief. We moved after a month to Looney Bay community housing. We are still living in the community housing unit assigned to us in 2006.

We applied for the Disability Support Program shortly after we settled at our new address. We also applied for employment in our professional sectors, in areas for high school students and for positions that required no educational qualifications. We wanted to make additional income regardless of the type of work. I was invited to an interview in September 2006 by the pest control division of the Multizone Department of Health. The result of the interview was not communicated to me after the promised two weeks. I stopped calling the personnel department to inquire about the outcome of the interview after a month of weekly calls that led nowhere.

I had received identical treatment from the same personnel department a few months before we left for the University of Shoreline in 1999. Luba and I quickly realized we were dancing to the same old music of employment denial and game playing by Multizonian employers. We have not applied for any other jobs since the rude and unprofessional treatment we received from the personnel department. We are guarding against another episode of humiliation and disrespect simply because we want to contribute to the advancement of knowledge in our respective areas of study.

CHAPTER 17
More Eye Problems

Another reason for my not being gainfully employed since March 2006, when we came back to Multizone, was the sudden and inexplicable recurrence of my eye problems. The problems started about a month after I stopped calling the personnel department. I had been receiving six monthly routine check-ups on my left eye from Dr. Ernest at the eye institute of the critical care wing of Looney Bay Hospital. At my request, Dr. Goodkind, who'd performed my cornea transplant surgery at the ophthalmology clinic of Grapevine University and Hospital, sent a copy of my file to Dr. Ernest.

The recurrence of the problems manifested as blurred vision and significant accumulation of floaters in my left eye. Needless to mention, I could not read with the eye, and the vision deteriorated to the point where I could barely see beyond arm's length. Several attempts by Dr. Ernest to treat the eye with medication were unsuccessful. In May 2009, when my family was in Redberry for our younger daughter Jael's wedding. I went and saw Dr. Goodkind and he was not pleased with the marked deterioration in my vision since he'd examined the eye prior to our departure to Multizone in March 2006. He'd performed cornea transplant surgery on my left eye in October 2001 and been able to restore 20/20 vision in the eye by 2006, when we left Redberry. He asked me about the type of follow-up care I had received in Multizone and suggested that surgical replacement of the vitreous humour in the back of the eye (a vitrectomy) might restore more vision in the eye. The lack of Grandonian medical insurance coverage for the expensive surgery coupled with the cost of accommodation and a lengthy period of recuperation and follow-up treatment made us decide against the surgical option. Dr. Goodkind chose the laser option instead. The outcome of the latter treatment was good enough to enable me to walk my daughter down the aisle and give her hand away in marriage.

In order to restore vision in the eye to a level that would enable me to read and perform more visual activities, Dr. Newton performed a vitrectomy on the eye at the surgical day care unit of the critical care wing of Looney Bay Hospital on August 25, 2010. I am currently under the care of Dr. Clemens, a cornea specialist, and Dr. Maria, an optometrist, who are members of the eye care group at Looney Bay Eye Clinic. I have regained substantial vision in the eye with the aid of a combination of a rigid gas-permeable contact lens and corrective glasses for reading and for distance vision. The correction is, however, not up to the point where I can drive an automobile.

CHAPTER 18

The Effect of Our Ongoing Ordeal: Glory to God

In this chapter, I will attempt to convey the painful physical, mental, psychological and social effects of being stripped of every human dignity and subjected to continuous stress on our family. It is unlikely people who are not in our shoes can grasp the full extent and pain of the horrific trauma. The ordeal is more than we can humanly bear. We attribute our survival to God's love and faithfulness to our family. The numerous accounts of God's intervention and protection that I mention are intended to be a source of hope, strength and faith building for whoever reads this book.

In addition to the tremendous psychological and physical damage the ordeal has inflicted on us, our careers, financial status and outlook for a bright and prosperous future have been seriously compromised. We are questioning the values and importance of medical ethics. On January 11, 1983, when I entered the University of Flatland Hospital to have knee surgery, I believed the physician would take care of me. By the same token, my wife believed she would be taken care of when she went into labour and went to the University of Flatland Hospital to have a baby on May 8, 1983.

Our expectations were to have my knee treated and have our daughter delivered safely, respectively. We trusted the doctors and believed they were capable of doing their duty. We committed ourselves to their care. So how did such evil happen to me and my daughter? My family's trust in the doctors and in the systems established to prevent or remedy such flagrant and unprovoked abuse of human rights and freedoms have been shattered into a million pieces like shrapnel from a powerful explosive.

Those doctors and others like them have violated, defaced and made a mockery of the sanctity of the Hippocratic oath taken by doctors. The words of this sacred oath include the following: "I will give no deadly medicine to anyone if asked, nor suggest any such counsel. But should I trespass and violate this oath, may the reverse be my lot."

The violation echoes in the ears of my wife and my conscience. We are always reminded that the reprobate mind presents a constant and continuous threat to society. Such mindsets would stoop to as low a level as possible to defile and violate the norms and tenets of a civilized society and culture.

We have become suspicious and even fearful of most hospitals. The aftermath of the trauma has forever affected our mental state and firm belief in the reliability of doctors. Every time we have to see a doctor in Multizone, we go through much mental anguish. The nagging and unavoidable question is this: Will I be taken care of or harmed? We are resisting the temptation to cast a broad net of blame and mistrust on all professional health practitioners; nevertheless, the trauma has clouded our perception and ability to be rational. The unresolved matter makes the question an agonizing one. Our fractured trust is not limited only to doctors. We are also plagued by a general mistrust of other professions and suffer from a withdrawal in interaction with human relationships. I will expound on the latter effect in a subsequent paragraph. All of us have developed health problems related to the ongoing trauma.

I am left with vision in only my left eye. In order to see through my left eye, I have to treat it daily with anti-inflammatory medication for the rest of my life. I still feel occasional pain and discomfort in the eye. The painful episodes last from four days to a week. At such times, the eye becomes sensitive to light, and I have to wear special dark glasses. I have to treat the eye at such times aggressively with multiple hourly anti-inflammatory drops and pressure-modulation drops until the pain subsides. My ophthalmologist gets involved in treating the eye when the pain and sensitivity to light persist for more than one week. I also have to replace the special gas-permeable lens in the left eye every two years at a cost of $150. For long-distance vision, I spend an additional $300 biannually on special glasses.

My wife is on antidepressants to be able to manage her depression and suicidal tendencies. She was hospitalized on four occasions for severe depression and mental breakdowns. In my opinion, she is not the vivacious and joyful woman I fell in love with and married. As the backbone of the family, she is enduring extreme suffering. Despite what is happening, she has been my indefatigable companion. She is firm and constant in supporting our expectation that justice will prevail.

Our first daughter, Naomi, turned 35 years old in May 2018. She did not graduate with a high school diploma and is functioning academically at a grade-5 level. She is unable to pick up and put down any objects, even objects as simple as her toothbrush, cutlery, a cup or a meal plate, without her hands shaking violently. She can hold objects when someone else places them in her hands. The constant task of placing and taking objects from her hands puts additional stress on my wife and me. A medical professional told me in confidence that she has scar tissue on the right lobe of her brain. Medical reports of two magnetic resonance imaging (MRI) scans on her brain do not mention the scars. We are eager to have another MRI examination repeated by a different medical facility. She also had frequent seizures as a child until she was 12 years old. We suspect the damage and injury to her brain occurred during the three days Luba was in the maternity ward after she delivered Naomi at the University of Flatland Hospital in Dusty Rose on May 8, 1983.

In previous chapters, I elaborated on our comments and the account of the treatment we received from the channels and authorities that deal with resolving injustice and awarding compensation. Briefly, all the attempts we made to put an end to the unjust acts were fruitless.

The immigration department in particular, along with other government agencies, was uncooperative and untrustworthy. We suffered a great deal under their authority. Their actions and decisions made the psychological damage more excruciating. The embassy of Nugget River also failed us. It became apparent to us that there was no one in the professional circle we could trust or turn to, at least not in Multizone.

Our inability to get help in resolving our ongoing ordeal and bring closure to the nightmare continues to inflict deep pain and family problems on our well-being. The ordeal has stripped away my profession as a scientist. It's been more than three decades since I earned my doctoral degree. The unresolved ordeal has prevented me from being productive academically, physically and financially. I was unable to provide for my children financially when they needed my support. I have hitherto not been able to provide for my wife. Pregnancy is meant to be one of the most beautiful times in a woman's life. Luba missed out on that beautiful and joyous celebration during her four pregnancies. Our lack of money denied her the pleasure of indulging in the delicacies and food that most pregnant women crave. She had to curb her cravings. Her maternity clothes were donated by neighbours and friends. She did not have the luxury of buying the styles of dress that would make her feel gorgeous about her changing body.

I have also not been able to contribute to the knowledge base in my field, as I had planned to do and would have been capable of doing. It is difficult and heart-wrenching for me to see my colleagues contribute to science and make successful careers and headway in life while I am receiving welfare cheques and disability stipends and struggling to make a livelihood.

The horrific trauma is like a millstone tied around our necks. It is difficult for my wife to perform her duties as a wife and mother and for me to perform my duties as a breadwinner. We are a traditional family. In my Kolaland culture, it is also my duty as the eldest son to take care of my aging parents because of the lack of any national social systems to cater to the needs of the elderly. My dad and mom passed away during our suffocating ordeal. A lack of money and the problems I was having with the Multizonian immigration authorities concerning my visa status prevented me from being present at their burials. Missing out on the sacred act of paying my last respects to my parents caused heart-wrenching pain. They passed away wondering why I was not around to take care of them. I am still dealing with the pain and guilt of my absence to this present day.

Luba's contribution was vital in holding the family together. Her education in family studies contributed greatly to our survival. Financially, it was tough to feed four young, rapidly growing children on the budget we were reduced to. Grocery shopping became a thing of ignominy. We felt resentment when watching other families walk out of the store with loads of groceries and with their children happily singing and jumping in anticipation of the abundance of yummy food and goodies. Most of the time, our grocery bill went over our budget, and Luba had to make a decision at the checkout counter on which food items to give back. An example would be a decision between a bag of potatoes and toilet paper.

For 35 years, we had no choice but to shop at thrift stores to buy clothes and household items. We look forward to the day when we can purchase new items. I remember the day our daughter Jael came home from elementary school frustrated and hurt. Her best friend had asked her why $3.99 was written under her shoes. Our children became too embarrassed to reply to such questions. My wife and I also felt uncomfortable and embarrassed when we met other parents who asked about our jobs and what we did for a living.

The children's high school years were not enjoyable for them. They felt our lack of money was the major contributor to their inability to participate in normal teenage activities and fun. They had no allowance for shopping, going to movies and dining out. Birthdays and Christmases were difficult for the family. The gifts they received came from their grandparents and the Salvation Army. My wife cried at all four high school graduations and longed for an end to the ever-lingering ordeal.

Three of our children have proceeded to college. Thank and praise God for guiding and directing their paths. The transition was not easy for them. Our son Zevin made this comment: "What is the use of higher education if our parents, after spending time attaining high degrees, are not benefiting from their efforts? It is discomforting to live in poverty for so long and observe other less educated people make progress in life, while Dad's high degree has come to nothing." Suffice it to say the children felt humiliated when they had to fill out loan applications. They had to give reasons why they needed financial assistance, and they felt it was demeaning to them to have to relate the story of our ordeal.

It was Luba's dream to decorate our home in a style exclusively for the Topas family. All the houses we had lived in were small in size for a family of six. We noticed that the lack of space and the constant close contact with each other created more tension among us. We had to live in low-income districts, usually surrounded by and exposed to drug and alcohol addicts and prostitution. It was not the environment we wanted to raise our children in. However, solid biblical teaching and grounding steered our children away from the social ills going on around them.

Summer vacations were a dreadful time for us. Our only escape was to walk around the neighbourhood. Try walking around a drug-infested neighbourhood year after year, and you will get a good taste of how dreadful it is. It was hard for the children to hear about their friends' vacations to exotic locations and fun-filled summer camps. Walking and city buses were our only means of transportation. The lack of a vehicle made family outings difficult. My hard-earned degrees have become redundant, and our dreams of living happy and productive lives have dissipated to the point of almost evaporating.

Our stress levels have developed to the extent that my wife and I argue daily and constantly. The resulting disturbance has brought the police and housing security to our house on numerous occasions.

The cause of our stress is primarily the lack of resources that would enable my wife and me to have normal lives and engage in the activities and programs every couple enjoys. We have not been on a honeymoon since we got married in December 1982. Our dinner dates are rare, almost non-existent. We are always together and feel as if we are prisoners of the crimes committed against me and my first daughter at the University of Flatland Hospital in Dusty Rose on January 11, 1983, and May 8, 1983, respectively. Thirty-five years of incarceration, except for the seven years we spent in Redberry is too long a life sentence for being a good and productive student.

The unjust imprisonment and denial of justice are unacceptable to us. The unjust treatment caused my wife to have four mental breakdowns between 1992 and 1998. She has also made one attempt at committing suicide. The periods of time she was in and out of the mental hospital were traumatic for me and our four children. Her psychiatrist advised her after the fourth breakdown to remain on medication for life. She takes her medications but does not like the side effects. One side effect is weight gain, and her mental state has forever been affected. It's a miracle she is able to function. The shattering and repeated breakdowns have resulted in memory loss. She also struggles daily to maintain a positive and happy mental state. The ongoing situation has hindered her efforts to get better.

The whole family has been under chronic stress for a prolonged period of time. In her article "The Stress Syndrome Solution," which appeared in the August–September 2007 issue of *Healthy Directions*, Dr. Michelle Honda, PhD, a noted holistic health practitioner, defined chronic stress as unresolved circumstances persisting over extended periods of time. She elaborated on the effects of chronic stress on the brain, hormones, sex and the circulatory system (heart, arteries and veins). Additionally, she pointed out that prolonged stress impedes the oxygenation process necessary to keep all the organs and the body as a whole functioning normally.

My family has exhibited and continues to exhibit most of the syndromes pointed out in Dr. Honda's article. It is particularly frustrating for us to know about the solutions and methods to manage these syndromes but to lack the resources to afford them.

The psychological effects of the ordeal have been evident in various forms in each member of my family. The statements our children wrote to my wife and me when we asked to know how they had been affected made Luba and me sad.

Generally, the psychological trauma has affected our interaction with people. The nagging question is this: Can we trust the person, or will he or she harm us? We are hesitant to get close to people because of our experience with betrayal. I became sick and disoriented and developed a fever that lasted for four days after being invited to a free lunch by a church friend. Additionally, we have confided in friends only to realize they were undermining our efforts to pursue justice.

The agonizing question of whom to trust is an ongoing game of guesswork in our minds. Our primary objective is to have the truth of the ordeal investigated. The investigation will be a first step in the process of our attempt to erase years of suffering and torment. It will be a much-needed and long-overdue step in regaining our peace of mind and developing trust in people and the system that has allowed these unjust and inhuman tortures to happen to an innocent family.

We have tried counselling, but it was not beneficial to us. Counselling, in our case, was equivalent to putting a bandage on a wound that needed sutures. We needed more than counselling. We want to have the cause of our ordeal investigated and dealt with in the proper way. We sought legal advice and made attempts to present our case in several courts of justice and have met with disdain, derision and fruitlessness. The most potent obstacle to making any progress in our ceaseless effort to regain freedom, normalcy, sanity and a purpose to continue to live is the lack of any concrete evidence to substantiate my accusation of unauthorized genetic experimentation during my knee surgery. We have made several attempts and pleaded with some noted genetic analysis experts and laboratories for help in DNA analysis. We know that a major obstacle to our efforts to have DNA fingerprinting analysis performed is interference from authorities who have political and bureaucratic clout. Our lack of money due to joblessness has also played a minor role in hindering our efforts.

Without the evidence, it is difficult for people to believe our story. We have experienced and observed similar patterns of doubt and disbelief from our extended families. They have not stood shoulder to shoulder with us to help us fight for our rights. We have, however, received financial support from close family members when we needed assistance to pay for our basic needs. Our family is still alone in trying to find a way through the political and bureaucratic maze we are faced with. The weight of the ordeal is too much for my family to bear. My family and I need to have closure to this painful and traumatic epoch of our lives. The needs of my daughter and I would be better met with proper legal and medical assistance. I have limited income and resources to pay for such help.

Our desire to know the truth is a right that all human beings are given by God and is entrenched in the constitution of Multizone. We have survived and are able to function as a family due mostly to our tenacious and unshakable faith in God. Our Christian friends, Bible study and church activities also contribute greatly to our survival.

Luba and I are grateful to God for the discipline and hard work that enabled three of our four children to graduate from university. All three of them are married and employed. We have also been blessed with seven grandchildren. Sadly, we have also lost two grandchildren. We are expecting two more grandchildren in October 2018 and January 2019. The most joyful part of our separation from our children when they were teenagers was that they did not lose their zeal and love for the Word of God. We are grateful to the pastors, congregations and godly friends who kept them close to God after we left them in Grandonia after I lost my position at the University of Shoreline in Redberry when my cornea perforated. All three of them are proactively involved in their churches. Their love for the Word of God is a testament to God's promise: "Train up a child in the way he should go: and when he is old, he will not depart from it" (Proverbs 22:6 KJV).

Another important lesson we learned after I lost my job is that God has a purpose in the things that happen in the lives of believers. Romans 8:28 says, "And we know that in all things God works for the good of those who love him, who have been called according to his purpose" (NIV).

Luba and I were initially frustrated and worried about leaving our children behind. Luba cried on several occasions when she could not deal with the thought of leaving our young children behind. I had to dig deep and call on God for strength and the words to console her. I cried a number of times also when Luba could not be consoled. I thank God for our ability to survive that particular sad and challenging time in our lives. It was particularly difficult for Naomi not to see her siblings. She wanted to go back to Redberry to join them. We puzzled about the relocation to Redberry and pondered whether it was a good decision. When the dust of our bewilderment and uncertainty settled, after much prayer, God revealed the blessings of the relocation to us.

We realized our association and involvement with the Gondwanan Christian Fellowship (GCF) in Redberry gave our children a solid ground on which to grow and mature in good biblical teaching. They also made the acquaintance of the teenage Christian children of professors, research fellows, graduate students and other non-academic members of the GCF. We attribute their excellent academic performance and admission to good schools to the discipline and co-operative learning habit of all GCF high school students. Most of the other students gained admission to good engineering, science, law, art and medical schools. Zevin earned an undergraduate degree in aerospace engineering from

Uniontown University. Jael completed her undergraduate studies in accounting at Shoreline University and concurrently earned her master's degree in accounting while working in Oil Town. Marko, our second son, graduated from Uniontown University with bachelor of science degrees in accounting and finance. Naomi made little progress in her academic work. She did not graduate with a high school diploma. Her performance was limited by her medical problems. We had good assessment of her condition, and we received excellent medical advice about her chances for employment. She made the acquaintance of some girls in her class and church groups. Some of those acquaintances have become good friends with whom she communicates often via telephone. She loves the Lord, and she is praying for a career in professional daycare or missionary work. All things are possible for those who believe and love God. Naomi adores being in the presence of God. We continue to expect a miracle for her healing.

Another aspect of God's faithfulness and purpose that we did not realize until later was the timing of my cornea problems and the treatment I received. Yes, the eye could have been treated in Multizone; nevertheless, we thank God for where my cornea perforated. Our distrust of Multizonian doctors at that time due to my knee surgery would have exacerbated my fear and worry about being treated in Multizone. Luba was also more relaxed. She was more involved in taking care of the family, and she even learned to cook delicious Gondwanan recipes. The ladies in the GCF insisted on teaching her how to prepare typical Ayama dishes. They told her, "You are married to an Ayama man, and we think Ayama meals will make him love you better." Luba laughed at the comment. She learned a few Ayama recipes—I think because she wanted to add to her collection of international recipes. She is an avid collector of foreign recipes. The children and I are lucky to be treated to her dishes. I think the Ayama ladies who taught Luba about Ayama cuisine believe in the adage "The way to a man's heart is through his tummy." I can testify that Luba's dishes lend much support to that adage.

The painful and destabilizing troubles with my eyes also revealed an important aspect of our marriage to me. Luba became the glue that held our family together in the midst of the confusion and trauma. Prior to my second successful cornea transplant, she served as my eyes and the children's anchor and source of strength as they tried to navigate through the maze of confusion and disappointment. She drove me to my appointments and held my hands to guide me to my doctor's clinic, our bathroom and everywhere in the house. She did all the grocery shopping and cooked for the family. She did everything to hold the family together. Her behaviour and actions made me grasp the true meaning of the biblical verse Genesis 2:18: "The Lord God said, 'It is not good for the man to be alone. I will make a helper suitable for him'" (NIV).

Additionally, she continues to honour her vows to be with me in sickness and in health. Luba drives wherever we have to go with a vehicle. I cannot drive due to my poor eyesight. I am eternally grateful to God for blessing me and our children with a woman who continues to fulfill the tenets of God's description of the wife of noble character in Proverbs 31:10–31 (NIV):

> A wife of noble character who can find?
> She is worth far more than rubies.
> Her husband has full confidence in her
> and lacks nothing of value.
> She brings him good, not harm,
> all the days of her life.
> She selects wool and flax
> and works with eager hands.
> She is like the merchant ships,
> bringing her food from afar.
> She gets up while it is still night;
> she provides food for her family
> and portions for her female servants.
> She considers a field and buys it;
> out of her earnings she plants a vineyard.
> She sets about her work vigorously;
> her arms are strong for her tasks.
> She sees that her trading is profitable,
> and her lamp does not go out at night.
> In her hand she holds the distaff

and grasps the spindle with her fingers.
She opens her arms to the poor
and extends her hands to the needy.
When it snows, she has no fear for her household;
for all of them are clothed in scarlet.
She makes coverings for her bed;
she is clothed in fine linen and purple.
Her husband is respected at the city gate,
where he takes his seat among the elders of the land.
She makes linen garments and sells them,
and supplies the merchants with sashes.
She is clothed with strength and dignity;
she can laugh at the days to come.
She speaks with wisdom,
and faithful instruction is on her tongue.
She watches over the affairs of her household
and does not eat the bread of idleness.
Her children arise and call her blessed;
her husband also, and he praises her:
Many women do noble things,
but you surpass them all.
Charm is deceptive, and beauty is fleeting;
but a woman who fears the LORD is to be praised.
Honor her for all that her hands have done,
and let her works bring her praise at the city gate.

The three weeks I was without sight in both eyes while I waited for cornea transplant surgery made me develop a keen appreciation for creation. I regained the sight in my left eye. The surgeons could not save the right eye. I am thankful and blessed to be able to see people, blue and even grey skies, the moon, stars, the sun, green grass, flowers, trees, insects, birds and the other living creatures. I realized I used to take a lot of things for granted. I never saw the need to be grateful and happy for God's gift of sight. When I lost and regained my sight, I became a new person. It is different when one is born blind or loses sight permanently at a young age before he or she can develop an appreciation for nature. When I lost the gift of sight, I could her Luba, my children, the chirping and singing of birds and the noises of nature and could mentally associate the voices and sounds with who and what was within earshot. The excruciating pain came from not being able to see them. When I regained sight, albeit in one eye, the joy, love and thankfulness I felt set me free from every feeling of hate, argument and dispute and all that is contrary to loving human beings and nature. The awareness of belonging and working for the common good and survival of all of God's creation awoke in me. I have stopped wasting precious time, sight, sound, taste, smell and touch. I indulge in all of these free and blessed gifts from God, and I am ever thankful. I can truly say that it is a waste of God's love to hate and destroy that which is here for us to enjoy. War, environmental pollution, racism and self-disrespect are all against God's purpose in creation.

Luba and I see God's purpose in all that is going on with our family. We understand now that the relocation to Shoreline was a part of God's ongoing plan for our family. The important lesson we learned is to always trust God and not rely on our own understanding. Indeed, we acknowledged God, and he is directing our path (Proverbs 3:5–6).

Currently, the family is divided between two great, God-loving nations. We are still glad and excited about God's guidance and provision for us. We have not given up hope and the expectation that we can amicably resolve this long and arduous chapter of our lives. Our God has preserved us and brought us this far. We believe that those who live in nations that profess freedom for all their citizens understand that the democratic principles and freedoms of a nation are meaningless until each and every citizen of that nation is given equal protection and justice. God has given and continues to give my family the opportunity to remain faithful and hopeful.

My wife and I can truly declare that God is good all the time. We cling to our favourite biblical verses, including Psalm 23, Psalm 91, Romans 8:28, Jeremiah 29:11, Malachi 4:2, Isaiah 40:31 and several other verses. Luba and I lean heavily on and derive strength from the words of the apostle Paul's messages to various churches and religious organizations, both foe and friend. We can truly identify with his message to the church in Corinth, to whom he wrote,

We are hard pressed on every side, but not crushed; perplexed, but not in despair; persecuted, but not abandoned; struck down, but not destroyed. We always carry around in our body the death of Jesus, so that the life of Jesus may also be revealed in our body. For we who are alive are always being given over to death for Jesus' sake, so that his life may also be revealed in our mortal body. So then, death is at work in us, but life is at work in you. (2 Corinthians 4:8–12 NIV)

It is my prayer that every believer and unbeliever who is going through trials and difficulties will continue to rely on and seek help from God.